Motivational and Sponsoring Skills for the Network Marketer

... an essential tool for the Network Marketer

by Jack Stanley

Printed in the United States of America

Chariot Press, Inc.
3030 Avenue E East
Arlington, Texas 76011

First Printing October 1995

ISBN 0-9649943-0-5

To Janet Mary

There would have been no book or, for that matter, no new life without you.

About Jack Stanley

As an internationally recognized motivational and sales training speaker, Jack has addressed groups ranging from 50 to 15,000 people in every major city in the United States and Canada. He also has had the pleasure of working with many large firms in both countries, including Fortune 500 companies.

Jack's speaking engagements have also taken him to the Virgin Islands, Puerto Rico, and Mexico. He and his brother own their own motivational and sales training company in Dallas, Texas.

Jack brings with him highly proven skills, techniques, and success principles that have made him one of the leading authorities on this subject in the country.

So sit back and enjoy one of the most rewarding, stimulating, and enlightening books that you will ever read!

Acknowledgements

Thoughts of love and fond memories of the following people who contributed to the completion of this book: Brothers Bill and Jim, Mom, Spray and Larry at Chariot Press, my distributor friends, and of course my wife, Janet.

Credits

Bill Stanley, Earl Nightingale, Dr. Denis Waitley, Dr. Wayne Dyer, Leonard Mednick, Mother Teresa, Bill Gates III, Charles Lindbergh, Jerry Boggus, Abraham Lincoln, and anyone else that I may have failed to mention.

Contents

They are carrying around and
trying to fulfill the wrong
mental picture of what it takes
to be successful.

Introduction

Have you ever wondered why some people are successful and others struggle their entire lives and never make it? Why does it seem so easy for some and so difficult for others? Could it be education, work ethic, time management, goal setting, energy, knowledge of the product or program, the ability to take action, luck, being at the right place at the right time, or just being born into? None of these are true reasons, nor are they satisfying because quite possibly you, like myself, have overcome some or all of these obstacles or barriers and still have not obtained the degree of success we desire.

The purpose of this book is to finally identify the true missing ingredients and help you reach your own personal goals. Because of my personal contact with literally thousands of people across the country who are seeking this same goal, I have come to one concrete conclusion. In most cases people are carrying around, and trying to fulfill, *the wrong mental picture of what it takes to be successful and to obtain their desired goals.*

Let me explain so that you can fully understand and appreciate the problem. I want you to create a

> # If you keep on doing what you've always done, you'll keep on getting what you've always got.

mental image in your mind of this thing called success and how you think it might be achieved. Got it? In most cases your mental image or picture will be totally wrong and inaccurate. So despite the fact that you may very well be living up to and, in fact, doing all the things that you consider necessary to obtain success, because your picture is wrong and inaccurate, you can never achieve it.

Bottom line... You have the wrong picture. For example, let's say that you want to become a professional golfer and you know that in order to do so you must master striking or hitting the ball with the various golf clubs, with a high degree of success and consistency. Let's also assume that you have a mental picture in your mind that you're suppose to hit the ball directly between your legs, striking the ball with a downward stroke, so that the ball actually travels between your legs. You and I both know that the ball is only going to travel ten or twelve yards. An advisor tells you to practice more, change your grip, think positive, be enthusiastic, work harder, but we both know that you will never be a good golfer hitting the ball in that fashion. Slogan to remember: *If you keep on doing what you've always done, you'll keep on getting what you've always got.* (Wrong results.) Let me give you an example of this. It's like looking for your automobile in the wrong parking lot. You can well imagine the feeling of frustration that would create. You come out of the store and know in your mind that you are in the right parking lot, so you set about looking for your car and you look and look, but you can't find it. Now, the average person would say to you, "Oh! Look harder! Be more enthusiastic! Approach it

A problem identified, is a
problem half solved.

with a positive mental attitude!" You and I both know you can do all these things, but if you are in the wrong parking lot you are never going to find your car. That is why success and achieving goals escapes so many. They are looking in the wrong places.

When we fall short, we are following and fulfilling the wrong set of plans or blueprints It would be difficult to build your dream home if you were building it from the wrong set of plans. The same holds true with sales people, or network marketers. Unless they are following the correct plan or blueprint, they will never achieve their final goal. As the saying goes, "A problem identified is a problem half solved."

The purpose of this book is to show you the *correct* things that you should be doing, or (let's put it another way) to paint you a picture puzzle of all the things that you must do to gain success, and then supply you with all the pieces of the puzzle to complete your picture.

The information in each chapter has been carefully selected to help guide you to become more successful. As you read this book, read it with a highlighter in your hand. While constantly taking a mental inventory of yourself, highlight any areas that strike a cord of special importance to you, or that you feel need extra work. This way, you can read and reread the highlighted areas over and over again. A key factor in reading and evaluating the information is being honest and truthful with yourself on weak areas. This is not the time to be dishonest with yourself. Remember, seek out new information such as you will find on these pages. You must first intellectually understand it, then

If you are not working on
yourself...you are not working!

New Information
First –
    Intellectually understand it.
Second –
    Psychologically accept it.
Third –
    Emotionally bond it to
    yourself.

physiologically accept, and finally, emotionally bond it to yourself, to where it is yours and it becomes a part of your being. When you have completed the book for the first time, because you have highlighted your areas, go back and reread and rework those areas as many times as necessary to make them yours.

A saying I would like to share with you and one that you should constantly keep in your mind for the rest of your life is: *"If you are not working on yourself...you are not working!"* If you are not continually working to improve yourself, to equip and push yourself to be the best human being possible, then you are not working on the correct project. It is a constant task to be your best. Each chapter, and the information it contains, is equally important to the others. They are, as a whole, dedicated to helping you build the best possible human being you can possibly be.

Good reading. Building a happy, beautiful life can be yours.

Jack Stanley

> People want to do business with an expert. It's what you add to the product that will justify the price.

Chapter One
Specialized Knowledge

"People want to do business with an expert."

It's what you add to the product that will justify the price. If the only thing you take to a customer is *product,* you can very well expect the objection *price* to come up quite often.

You must add value to the product with your specialized knowledge of that product or plan. The product or plan will *not* sell itself, no matter how good it is or how good the company is. That's what success is all about—turning yourself into an expert on your product line or network plan. For you to become highly successful in this or any other endeavor, you must equip yourself with certain procedures that you must acquire, and principles that you must practice. This holds especially true in the selling profession and in network marketing.

The first key to success is *specialized knowledge.* Remember, people want to associate themselves with successful and knowledgeable people. People who are seeking success look to someone, such as yourself, who is on the path to success, or has acquired a certain

Success leads to success.

Trust—Empathy—Creditability.

People want to associate themselves with successful and knowledgeable people.

Everyone's looking for some-one that is creditable.

degree of success, because most people know that *success leads to success.*

Specialized knowledge means an in-depth knowledge about your product or program. You must acquire three things from a customer or a prospect that you are trying to sponsor into your network: *trust, empathy,* and *credibility.* Specialized knowledge falls into the category of credibility. You have to know your product or program inside and out. You have to be able to anticipate every question that your client may present to you, and answer it to their complete satisfaction in a truthful and convincing matter. If at any time your answer does not come across as credible or truthful, doubt springs up in your prospect or customer's mind. You are then further away from turning that person into a customer, friend, client, or an associate in your organization. Credibility. Everyone is looking for someone who is credible.The only way to obtain that knowledge is to seek it out—about your program or your product line. Understand one thing. This responsibility rests totally on your shoulders. I have had the pleasure and experience to interview many young, prospective sales people. Many times during the interview the young salesperson will say "Yes, I believe that I can be successful, if I'm given the knowledge and information, and perhaps if they send me to a training program." And I would like to say to them, "Young man (or lady) that responsibility rests almost entirely on your shoulders if you truly want success."

First, let's talk about a product that you may be interested in selling in your program. Later, we will come back and talk about the program or plan. If you

The customer is more
interested in benefits
than features.

"What's in it for me?"

want to be successful in selling a product, you have to know all about that product. You have to know exactly what it is designed to do and not to do. Many times I've seen sales-people get carried away with their adjectives and descriptions of the benefits and features of a product and their presentation becomes exaggerated. They start making statements about what the product will do that falls totally short of what the product was designed to do; therefore, in the customer's mind, they are disappointed when it doesn't perform to their expectations. Know *exactly* what the product is designed for, its application, how it can be used, and its features and benefits. And when you explain the product to the customer, keep in mind that the customer is more interested in *benefits* than features. Many times salespeople get hung up on describing features of a product when in reality they should be showing the customer *how it will benefit him or her.* When you are presenting a product, always ask yourself this mental question. This is also what the customer across the table from you is thinking. "How is this product going to benefit me?" Or, to put it more bluntly, *"What's in it for me?"* You have to answer that question to their complete satisfaction. Where are you going to get this *specialized knowledge* on a product? First, take the product and work, experiment, and examine it. Read the directional label or information sheet. Gather all the information about that particular product, so that you fully and totally understand it yourself. Remember, people are looking for people who know what they are talking about. Put the information into presentation form, figuring out what the important points are, and stressing them.

Nothing sells itself.

"What you are
thunders so loudly,
I hear not what you say."

People buy
good presentations.

I want you to take this into consideration. When presenting a product or program to your customer, remember that they will not sell themselves. I've heard many people say, "You know, we have such a fine company we represent, that the products should sell themselves." Well, nothing sells itself. It's what you add to the product that will enhance its value to the customer. Let me explain that a little bit more. If the only thing you take to the customer is the product, plan, or service itself, then you can very well expect the objective *price.* However, if you take specialized knowledge about your product or plan to your customer, in-depth information. in-depth credibility coming from you, and the ability to understand that product by explaining it fully, if the conviction is in your voice and in your heart, the customer will feel it. Many times it's not so much what you say to the customer, but what he or she is feeling from you. As Emerson said, *"What you are, thunders so loudly, I hear not what you say."* Make sure you have a professional presentation ready. Work on it. Pick out the good strong points about your product or plan and stress those. It's how you make your presentation that makes the difference. It's what *you* add to the product or plan that enhances that products value. Products or services do not sell themselves. People buy good presentations. To be successful, you must become a professional presenter. Think of it this way. What if you were on television and had sixty seconds to tell all the good strong points about the product or plan? In that atmosphere and climate, you would have to be exact, precise, and have a beginning, middle and end to your presentation. You'd hit your strong points or high points right where you needed them the

"Information is power."

People want to become
creditable.

most, in the closing part of the presentation. That's what I'm suggesting here. Many times we get sloppy and come to the table ill prepared to make a truly professional presentation. This chapter is designed to turn you into a professional salesperson, a professional presenter, and the only way you can do this is have in-depth knowledge about your product or plan.

Remember, *"Information is power."* the more information you have, the more powerful you come across, and people look up to that. They want to associate with, feel, and be part of that power. That's what presenting knowledge is all about. You have the ability to do this. This is the easy part of your trip to success. Gather the knowledge, put it into a presentation form so that people can receive the information favorably, and allow them to understand it and feel that you know what you are talking about. *Credibility.* People want credibility. People want to become credible. So many times we get lazy in seeking out the information about our product and it comes across that way. Know that when you have this knowledge within yourself and the ability to communicate it, there is an aura that comes off of you that your customer can feel subconsciously. Many times it's not so much what you say as what the customer is feeling from you. We will discuss this more in Chapter Three. Yes, in-depth and specialized knowledge is one of the vital tools to any success.

Now, let's talk about your *network plan*. If you are truly interested in building your network you must know every detail of how it works. If you need to sketch it out on an easel or a piece of paper, do it first in front of a family member to eliminate your mistakes.

Remember to do it their way.

Success leads to success.

Next, ask yourself this question, "How much do *you* really know about your network plan?" Why should anyone be sponsored by you or associate themselves with you in your organization, if they don't feel that you are the most equipped and knowledgeable person in that field or network? Put yourself in the prospect's chair. This falls into the empathy category. Realize that your prospect has a lot of anticipation, anxieties, questions, and fears; the first thing they want to know is, what is this all about? How do I relate to this program or plan? You have to know how it works and if your upline or the person that sponsored you has a distinct way to present the program or plan. Do it their way, because obviously they have been successful. They have got something that they know will work for you. *Remember to do it their way,* but do it with yourself in it, heart and mind. Yes, success leaves clues, but you have to equip yourself with knowledge. If your upline was not as good as what you thought they could have been in their presentation to you, say to yourself, "I can do that better. I can enhance that. I can improve that presentation. I can help my client see the value and how it will benefit them, their lives and their families." That's what people are looking for: knowledgeable people who know what they are talking about and how to explain it. *Success leads to success.*

The third area where we need to gather specialized knowledge and information, and perhaps the most important area, is the customer or prospect themselves. We need to learn what their goals, dreams, and motivations are. Look at the situation from his or her point of view. Why should the customer or prospect take an interest in you or what you are proposing, if

The best way to get people to take an interest in me, is to take an interest in them first.

"The sin of the obvious."

Find out what the prospect's motives, dreams, and desires are.

you have not taken enough time to seek out additional information about him or her? I have found in life, the best way to get people to take an interest in you, is to take an interest in them first. You have to seek out information about the prospect you want to sponsor into your network. Find out what their family consists of, the names of their spouse and children, their ages, what their goals and dreams are. Remember, whatever motivated you in the beginning to get into a network plan may not be the same motivating factor for your prospect. I call it "the sin of the obvious." Don't assume that because we know our own background, motives, dreams, and desires that everyone else has similar ones. That's just not true. We have to search out and really interview that prospect to find out exactly what's going on in his or her heart, mind, and soul. Find out what the prospect's motives, dreams, and desires are, and then when you make your presentation incorporate all of those objectives in your presentation. In other words, paint a picture in your presentation to fulfill your prospect's individual goals and dreams. We can't put everyone under the same umbrella, because what appeals to you and I, may not appeal to someone else. You must paint a picture that fulfills *their* dreams and goals. To do that you must seek out *specialized knowledge* about that particular person—what they want out of life, where they want to go, and how they would like to achieve financial freedom. By seeking out such specific information you can really customize your presentation to fit that prospect. One mistake I want to caution you on, is that a person may make too good a presentation. Sometimes the presentation may be unbelievable for

If it sounds too good,
it's probably too good
to be true.

$$C + B = A$$

"I can see myself doing that!"

that prospect and he or she cannot accept it mentally.

Let's say we were talking to a young couple. Maybe they have worked together their entire married life and had an income of $25,000 to $45,000 per year. It's taken them maybe twelve years to get there. Now here you are making a presentation to them. Painting such a glorious picture of all this money they are going to make, all this free time that they are going to have, and this large downline they will have working for them. If it sounds too good, it's probably too good to be true in their minds. Remember, if it sounds too good to be true, it generally is. I'm not saying that these people can't do everything that you are suggesting, but it's hard for them to conceive it. If they can't conceive it, they can't believe it. If they can't believe it, they are never going to achieve it. That's the old formula that I have always used—$C+B=A$. Your prospect has to be able to conceive what you're proposing, (C), and believe that he or she is capable of doing it (B), in order to achieve it (A). That's the whole key. Customize your presentation to fit each person's individual needs, desires, and wants, but don't make it too big or too small. Fill the picture they carry around in their mind and all at once they will say to themselves, "I can see myself doing that." If they can see themselves doing it, they will. If they can't see themselves doing it, they won't and they will not sign up with you. The whole key in making a presentation is to fit that individual person's belief patterns and past experiences. It is one of the most vital areas that you have, to gather knowledge and information on your prospect. Because God made every one of your prospects different and unique, paint the picture to fit your prospect's

Paint the picture to fit your
prospect's dreams.

Specialized knowledge is
one of the important keys
to success.

dreams. This specialized knowledge and information is one of the important keys to your success.

To summarize the importance of this chapter let me relay to you a story that my brother Bill shared with me. On one of his many trips to the main public library in downtown Dallas, he observed many street people and unemployed people lounging, loafing, and sleeping on the sidewalks around the library. The irony of it all is, whatever these people needed to be gainfully employed and to become a valuable citizen was just on the other side of that library door. *Knowledge. Specialized knowledge* is one of the important keys to success.

Their mind quite possibly could say yes, but their physical body says no.

Chapter Two
Energy

The second key to success in any adventure, endeavor, or career is *energy*. You have to have energy and an excitable level of energy to truly succeed.

Let's stop and think about it. You have equipped yourself with knowledge of the program and know it inside and out. You also have customer knowledge, specialized to fit individual needs and desires.

Now my question to you is, do you have the energy to take it to the marketplace? Interestingly enough, a tremendous number of salespeople in all aspects of business are knowledgeable and well-equipped to be successful. Yet, sadly, they cannot go into the marketplace nor maintain a selling level of energy for a prolonged time, which would allow them to be successful. Their minds quite possibly could say "yes, let's go and do it," but their physical body says "no" and just shuts them down. Wouldn't it be a shame if you had all this knowledge but not the energy to be successful? This is what stops many people from being truly successful in networking or any other business

> # Do you have the physical and mental energy to take it to the marketplace?

or athletic event. Many times the only difference between a buying and a non-buying presentation is the energy level put into it by the presenter or would-be sponsor.

You have to ask *yourself,* since you have obtained this information do *you* have the physical and mental energy to take it to the marketplace? One of the most common traits of the successful people I have come in contact with in my life is energy. They have an extremely high level of energy, which allows them to perform their duties above and beyond what would be normally expected of them. This holds particularly true for network marketers because, in most cases, they start their second career from a first job or first career basis. Therefore, they have to work during the day at their regular job, then build their network or business after hours. *Energy* is truly a vital key to their success.

Let's talk about different areas of the world where energy really takes precedent over anything else. Think about someplace where energy plays a vital part in not only succeeding, but in just surviving. What about the wild animal kingdom? It has always been the rule that the strongest, most able, and energized survive. Out in the forest, predators must be energized to catch their prey. Birds must have energy to keep themselves aloft. In athletics, many times the results are decided in the final moments of the contest. It's the team that is in the best physical condition that actually prevails and becomes the winner. Most football and basketball games are decided in the last two or three minutes of the last quarter. Could it be that one team

Let's call your body
your taxi cab.
How well are you taking care
of your taxi cab?

or individual is in better physical and mental condition than his opponent? I think so. That also holds true for people in the business world. The one common denominator or golden thread that appears to run through all successful people is that they possess a high level of energy.

As prospects or entrepreneurs in the network marketing system, we also must obtain this winning energy level. Think about it this way. you have a physical body that is taking you on your journey through life. Let's call your body your taxi cab. How well are you taking care of your taxi cab? You can only be as successful and go as far as your taxi cab will take you. Many times we actually take better care of our cars, homes, and toys than we do ourselves. Maybe you hadn't thought about it before, but most contests in life come down to not only the mental but also the physical aspects of your preparation. I suggest we start taking care of ourselves. We should start with what we put into our bodies as far as food and drink are concerned. Also, think about an exercise program. I don't mean that you have to be an Arnold Schwarzenegger, but after consulting your doctor, consider walking, jogging or a sport activity such as racquetball, tennis, bicycling, or swimming. What I'm strongly suggesting, is that you need to get into physical condition to work at a high level of energy and thereby excel. A survey was taken in this country some years ago and it was found that most salespeople are physically tired by about 1:30 or 2:00 in the afternoon. Now here's the interesting part. They go through the motions and say to themselves, "I'm making my calls and doing the things that I should be doing," but my question to

There is a winning presentation
and a losing presentation

I'm physically tired so I must
produce excuses to justify
my actions.

them would be (and my comment to you is)—are they really executing at a high level of energy? You can go through your presentation okay, but there is a winning presentation and a losing presentation. Many times it comes down to just one factor: the level of energy that you put into it, which will ensure your success.

Sometimes your mind will self-talk to you, subconsciously. Let's say it's one-thirty in the afternoon and all at once, in the self-talk process of your thoughts, you start sending messages to yourself. "Gee, I don't know if I want to go across town. Traffic's pretty bad," "I don't think that prospect will be there to see me," "maybe I'd better stop and get my car washed," or, "my wife did ask me if I had a chance, to stop and get some milk and bread before I go home." What are you doing to yourself here? You're making excuses, subconsciously, not to make that call. But why? Because you are physically tired and consciously you're not aware of it. In other words, what you're saying to yourself is, "I'm physically tired, so I must make excuses to justify my actions for not making that sales call." That's what we must be aware of.

Let's talk about network marketers. I've heard people talk about a good idea or plan that they wish to accomplish for that evening. They're going to have an appointment with, or call on this individual, or they're planning to attend a meeting. They get home, have dinner, and then sit in front of the television set and say, "you know, I think I'll put that off tonight. "Sometimes they don't even recognize that they're physically or mentally exhausted; therefore, they compromise themselves because of their condition. We have to guard

**"Winners do what
loosers won't."**

Winners will go that extra mile.

against that and take action. We must be physically capable of carrying out our plans and goals to accomplish everything we want to do in our network marketing career. Sure, it's difficult, but if it were easy, everyone would do it. *"Winners do what losers won't."* Everyone has different goals and dreams, but winners will go that extra mile and put in that extra hour or two in the evening. Winners will make the time to do it. Losers are people who don't have that intense desire and will just cop out and say, "no, I'll tell you what, I'm just a little bit too tired this evening. I can't do it. I'll put it off until tomorrow." We have to be careful of that. We must be energized. We have to watch our diet. In many cases, people are eating the wrong types of food and loading their bodies (or taxi cabs) down. Many times in a sales or plan presentation, the only difference between a customer nodding yes or shaking his head no is the energy level of the presenter. Many times it's what they feel coming off you that excites them.

Let's come back for just a moment to the world of athletics. Think about a professional, college, or high school basketball team. Probably the best athletes in the world are basketball players. Are the players out on that court superbly conditioned? In most cases the answer is yes. Think about hockey players. Can you imagine skating up and down that rink for the full three periods? Think about professional football players. They play sixty minutes, running up and down the field. All of these athletes have high energy levels. Let's go to another example. I'm a baseball fan, and many times I've seen a batter hit a ball to the outfield and, in the process of running the bases, he gets all

It's very difficult to obtain your goals when you have a low energy level.

Take care of this taxi cab that's going to take us through life.

tired out. The ball is thrown to third and he gets tagged out, because he actually had to slow down. I'm not criticizing baseball players, but I am saying that these players could be in better condition because so many times they can't even run the bases, which are only ninety feet apart. The lack of conditioning and energy is what amazes me.

Professional salespeople and network marketers truly have to be in condition to take their plan, dreams, and goals to the marketplace to make themselves successful. It's very difficult to obtain your goals when you have a low energy level. How do we get a high energy level? We exercise. Consult your doctor, then put yourself on a moderate program initially. Something simple that you can do. Watch what you eat and drink. To be successful we have to get in good physical condition. We're not trying to be athletes, but we are trying to be successful human beings, which requires us to be healthy and take care of this taxi cab that's going to take us through life. It's the only taxi cab we will ever have. You've heard it said many times, "this body is our temple that will take us through life." We want to have the best quality of life, and it would be so sad if we were able to obtain our goals, freedom, and the riches of life, but not have the physical quality of life to enjoy it. That's why one of the main goals each and everyone of you should have is to get yourselves physically fit, so that you can enjoy your life and the journey through it. From the animal world of nature, to the athletic world, to the professional world, *energy* is a vital key to success.

It's a constant journey to develop yourself into the

Work on yourself to be the ultimate human being that you can become.

That's a pretty tall task!

very best, not only salesperson, but the best person you can become. If you continuously work on yourself to be the ultimate human being that you can become, the world will seek you out and reward you with success. It is a step by step development of yourself in all aspects of your life, *career. family, spiritual* and *physical development.*

You may have asked yourself, or maybe the thought may have come to you as you've read this chapter, "that's a pretty tall task! I've got to get myself in physical shape, be able to work for eight to ten hours a day and be professional in my presentation, every sales call?" Let me see if I can put your mind at ease just a little bit. I don't want you to think that this is an insurmountable job. It's not. It is a constant development and self-improvement program, and the only way you are going to gain success is to become the very best human being you can become. When you do, people will seek you out, want to associate and be in business with you.

You may ask yourself this question "do I have to do this energizing for the rest of my life?" The answer is yes, but to a certain degree. Let's see if I can give you a more accurate and acceptable answer. When I started as a salesman covering the state of Michigan, I was selling a line of maintenance chemicals through a national, private-label company with corporate offices in Chicago. In Michigan at that time there was little customer base. My job as a salesman was to go into that new territory and build a base. In this type of sales, once you get that base built and service them, they would remain your customers and give you

Put it into high gear, into overdrive.

repeat orders. That's what you're always looking for as a salesperson: A residual type of business that will bring reorders in. Salespeople have a difficult time making a living selling a product that doesn't repeat. An example would be an automobile salesman; their customers are only going to buy a new car every second or third year, many even longer than that. Unless they build a huge customer base they cannot survive. Maintenance chemicals repeat almost on a monthly basis, but first, I had to energize myself to build the customer base. Working on a commission structure, if you didn't sell, you didn't earn anything. I had to raise my level of energy to work at the highest peak of performance that I knew how. I studied and tried to improve myself, working on all aspects of salesmanship, human development, and personal growth, so that I could obtain a good customer base. I worked hard and energized for the first two or three years of my new career. I don't believe I could have maintained that schedule for the rest of my life. However, I knew that once I got my customer base established, servicing and building rapport with them, they would remain my customers. In fact, they not only remained my customers, but become even better customers for me. *This* is what I'm asking you to do for the first two or three years of your career. Put it into high gear, into overdrive. Work yourself at a higher level to establish your customer base, which would be your network. I'm not saying that you can shut everything down after that. You can't. But I am saying that you can shift into a little lower gear to *maintain and work what you have.* But you have to get that customer base established before you can do that. Most people go through

God doesn't care how many
seeds you plant.

their entire lives in a very low gear, so, consequently, they never establish any type of base about themselves, or about whatever they're trying to sell or build. That's what I'm sharing with you. Let's work hard for the next two or three years of our lives, so we can enjoy the fruits of our reward for years to come.

It's almost like the farmer planting his field. He has to go into his field and plow, till, cultivate, plant the seeds, fertilize, and weed it. Then when harvest time comes and he has done all that he should have, he will truly reap the rewards of a great harvest. That's what we want to do with our lives. We want to plant and take care of a lot of seeds, doing it with a high energy level. God doesn't care how many seeds you plant, that's the great thing. He doesn't care whether you plant a square yard or acres of seeds. It all depends on you and your level of energy and knowledge.

Now then, in network marketing, we all know that to establish this core of 75 to 125 people, it will take a lot of energy and knowledge. However, once we get to that level and continuously do our job working within the framework of these people, our future growth is assured. It's getting that first 75 to 125 people in our network established. Once we do, our seeds of greatness and future growth are right there.

If I haven't convinced and eased your mind yet, I'd like to share one more example that is just so obvious to me. I fly almost every week of my life to some destination in North America to put on a seminar, or workshop, or to give a speech. The plane I take and its ability to fly amazes me. For example, a 747 has anywhere between 200 to 300 passengers on it, all carrying

He pulls the flaps in, throttles
back on the engines, and lets
the plane cruise.

Then watch it fly!

at least two pieces of luggage each. When the plane gets fully loaded, God only knows what it weighs, but for that pilot to get it off the ground, and in the air he has to use all the power, and thrust that those engines can generate. Those engines are putting out the maximum amount of force that they were designed for to lift that plane off the ground, into the air, and up to the cruising altitude. Every bit of energy that can be generated is used. However, once the pilot gets the plane to cruising altitude, what does he do? He pulls the flaps in, throttles back on the engines, and lets the plane cruise. Does he fly full throttle at his cruising altitude? No. He gets to the proper altitude and lets the plane cruise. That's not all that different from what we are talking about in your career. Put all the energy that you can generate into getting your career off the ground and into the air, then you can cut back and start enjoying. But you can't cut back at the start-up time, or until you get your career to a certain plateau or level, which does not mean we are going to shut everything down and quit working. If you quit working, you quit growing, and you start dying. We have to grow and improve, continuously, but at the start of your career you must energize to get it off the ground and into the air. *Then* watch it fly!

"The quality of life is in direct proportion to the quality of your communication with yourself and other people."

Chapter Three
Rapport and Communication

I believe the subject of this chapter is the most intriguing, interesting, fascinating, and useful of all the keys to success.

Let's begin by defining this word *rapport*. What exactly does it mean and, more importantly, what does it mean to you in your success? Rapport means that you are in sync with another person—have similarities, or commonalities, are on the same wave length, or have similar viewpoints. *Communication* and the ability to communicate with other people and how it's going to affect your life. I can best share this thought with one statement, and I'd like you to read this statement many times.

The quality of your life is in direct proportion to the quality of your communication with yourself and other people.

Take the first part of that last statement—"communication with yourself." We all know that we communicate with ourselves through our thoughts, our self-talk to ourselves in quiet time, meditation, and even in our dreams. The question I have to ask you is,

Just say to yourself "stop!"
You haven't given yourself
permission to talk to yourself
that way.

what have you been saying to yourself in your thoughts? Are your thoughts positive or negative? Many times people destroy or retard their success by their own overly negative thoughts. Think back on the day. What do you say to yourself? Are you saying things such as "Yes, I'm going to be successful," or do you say "I don't believe I can do this. I've not been successful in the past, why do I think I should be successful now? I don't know if I can sell that product. I don't know if I can sponsor that person into my network." I often wonder why we say these things to ourselves. Earl Nightingale came out with a magnificent tape many years ago called *The Strangest Secret*. The strangest secret was as Earl said, "we become what we think about." What he says on his tape, is that thoughts become tangible things. The things that we believe and the things that we think in our mind will actually manifest themselves in our real life. If that's the case, and I truly believe this is so, then why not think good, positive, prosperous thoughts? If this really is true, and we are going to manifest something in our life, let's manifest something good, pleasant, prosperous, healthy, and spiritual. Let's not think of anything negative. Marty Seldman has an excellent tape out called *Self Talk*. In his tape he gives a great exercise on this. When negative thoughts come into your minds he says, just say to yourself "stop!" Call out your name—whatever your name is—you haven't given yourself permission to talk to yourself that way. Do you realize that many times we say things to ourselves, in our minds, that we would never allow another human being to say to us in person. For example, if someone met us on the street and said, "Jack, you're not going

I don't say walk away
anymore, I say run!

Your mind will manifest what
your thoughts are.

to be successful. You're not going to do well in this network marketing plan. You're not going to sell those products. You're not going to make any money. What in the world are you thinking?" You would dismiss that person and tell him to get out of your way. You know he has no right to say those things to you, and yet we say these things to ourselves in our thoughts. We have to stop this terrible habit. As Marty says, we have to say stop! And not allow ourselves to talk to ourselves this way. When a negative thought enters your mind, erase it. I've used this expression for many years—when you come in contact with a negative person in your life, I used to say walk away from that person. I don't say walk away anymore, I say *run!* Get away from anyone that's negative. That includes yourself. If you're negative, turn yourself around and stop thinking that way. *Remember, your mind will manifest what your thoughts are.* We have to put good thoughts into our mind, so that good things will come into our lives.

The second part of communication is how well you communicate *with other people.* Or, to put it another way, do you communicate with people in a selling or sponsoring posture, the way those people communicate with themselves? So many times, we talk to people and communicate with people, the way we talk and communicate with ourselves and it falls on deaf ears. You've heard people say, "I just talked to so-and-so, gave him a sales or sponsoring presentation, and I honestly don't believe he heard a word I said." You may be absolutely correct. You are not communicating with that person the way that person communicates with himself. That's what we need to learn in this chapter—how to *communicate* with people the way

We communicate with people
in three basic ways.

Be aware of fluff words, and
don't use them.

they communicate with themselves. Remember the following two important points:

1. The quality of your life is in direct proportion to the way you communicate with *yourself* and

2. How you communicate with *other people.*

Then people can receive your message favorably and nod their head yes when you ask for the order or signed application.

We communicate with people in three basic ways:

1. The words we speak

2. The tonality of our voice

3. The physiology of our body

Let's start with #1, the words you speak in your presentation for a sale, or to join your organization. The *words* represent only about seven to ten percent of the message you are trying to get across. Of the message you are trying to convey to a prospect or customer, he will only receive seven to ten percent of that message in the words you speak. For this reason you must choose exact, specific, and believable words. Try to expand your vocabulary. It doesn't have to be perfect, but at least have a good enough vocabulary to pick and choose the exact words that you want to use in your presentation, knowing that your prospect is only going to receive seven to ten percent of the whole message in those words. Next, to be aware of *fluff words,* and don't use them. A fluff word is a word that could have several different meanings, depending upon the listener. An example would be the word "great." What's great to you may be just "good" to someone else.

Watch the tone, tempo, speed, clearness, volume, and the colloquialisms that you use in your presentation.

As you read this chapter, remember what the objective here is to communicate with people. You want them to receive your message favorably. If you are trying to sponsor an individual, remember, he is mentally painting a picture in his mind, based on your ability to communicate with him the way he communicates with himself. Remember, the words you speak only represent a small part of the total picture that you are trying to implant in his mind about the value of your presentation.

The second way people receive information, and even more important and valuable than the words that you speak, is the *tone or tonality of your voice.* Many times people will draw a conclusion based on the tone in which you are expressing yourself. In fact, the tone of your voice has about five times more favorable impact than the words that you speak. As much as 35 percent to 40 percent of a person's decision will be made based on the tone of your presentation. We will expand on this later, but remember, you must use the *prospect's tone* that is the tone he uses in his self-talk. You are trying to get him to receive your information the way he brings information in to the decision maker, his mind. From now on watch the tone, tempo, speed, clearness, volume, and the colloquialisms that you use in your presentation, making sure they all match your prospect's. I'll explain this more as we go on, but the tone of your voice is extremely important in communicating your message to your customer, so that he in turn, at the conclusion of your presentation, nods his head yes, because you are on his *communication* channel.

If I can get the individual I'm trying to sponsor into my network to connect with me, I am on the golden bridge of opportunity.

The third way, and even more important than the first two ways, is by the *physiology of your body* as you make your presentation. Physiology—don't confuse it with body language. In fact, I don't believe in body language. Physiology means your hand and body movements, your gestures, mannerisms, the raising of your eyebrow, and the tilting of your head. The physiology of your body actually represents about 50 percent to 55 percent of your capacity to communicate with your prospect. He or she will tune into the physiology of your body to see if it coincides with his own thought patterns and body movements. From now on, take note of your customer's physiology, body movements, mannerisms, gestures, eyebrows, head movements, and so on. In making your presentation, mirror back to the physiology of his body. Remember, the success you achieve is going to be directly proportional to your ability to communicate with people or prospects, in such a manner that they receive the information that you are trying to convey and at the end of your presentation they have a complete and comfortable picture of you and your proposal. That's your objective.

Now, let's go back to the word *rapport*. The synonym I like is *connect*. If I can get the individual I'm trying to sponsor into my network to *connect* with me, I am on the golden bridge of opportunity of bringing that person into my organization. If that person doesn't connect with me they will not be sponsored by me, so the word connect is extremely important. To me, the word rapport means that I have to build, in that prospect's mind, a golden bridge between him and myself. I have a theory I believe it to be absolutely

> # Talk about his goals, interests, and desires.
>
> ## I think likes attract.

true. I call it my *thousand to one theory.* My theory is that people tend to like themselves a thousand times more than they like anyone else, including you or me. Think about yourself and your prospect. I believe you'll agree that he tends to like himself about a thousand times more than he likes you. There's nothing wrong with that. That's the way God made us. Why do I bring up this point? For this reason, when you're in front of a prospect you wish to bring into your organization, why in the world do you talk about yourself and your accomplishments? That prospect is not interested in you or me. Who is he interested in? Himself. Therefore, talk about *his* goals, interests, and desires. He is not as much interested in what you have accomplished as what he has accomplished. He is sitting and listening to you and your presentation and trying to figure out how is this going to benefit him or what's in it for him.

Let's talk now about building *rapport* remembering what we have just learned and accepted. You have always heard that opposites attract. If that's the case, opposites would attract and build *rapport.* I don't believe that to be true at all. I think *likes attract.* Think about yourself. Don't you like to be around someone like yourself? Think about your best friend or your spouse. Why did you marry your spouse? Is it because that individual has somewhat similar characteristics and values? For example, say that you go out for an evening, attending a party. Let's say you're a quiet, reserved, soft-spoken type of person. You walk into the party and over in one corner you hear some people who are having a loud, robust time, laughing, hooping and hollering. As you walk into the room

This golden bridge of opportunity called rapport has been established.

Mirroring and Matching.

your natural instinct is to get *away* from that group of people, because they are *different* from you. No right or wrong here, it is just that they are different. You are not attracted to those individuals. Therefore, I don't believe that opposites attract. I believe *likes* attract. *The more you are like me, the more I will like you.* You see, I like myself a thousand times more than I like anyone else, and if I see something in you that reminds me of myself, liking myself, I will like you. Show me someone who likes Jack Stanley and I'll show you a very high closing ratio. Show me someone who doesn't like Jack Stanley and I cannot *give* them the program or service that I am selling. Also remember, *the more you are dislike me, the more I will dislike you.* If I dislike you, I want nothing to do with you and I will certainly not be sponsored by you nor buy your product. The more you are like me, the more I will like you.

Now, I have another challenge for you. How do we get these people to like us? Are we just going to seek out people who are similar to us? The answer is no. Because the world is made up of several different categories of people, we have to think of some way to meet the challenge of how to get different people to see something in us that reminds them of themselves, knowing full well that they like themselves a thousand times more than they like anyone else. If they can see something in us that reminds them of themselves, all at once this golden bridge of opportunity called *rapport* has been established. People want to be around people who are similar to themselves. The whole key to success is based on this premise. How do we do it? It's a method called *mirroring and matching* the

If he speaks softly, I want you to
speak softly.

I want people to see
something in you that reminds
them unconsciously
of themselves.

individual as we interview them and present our program. What do I mean by mirroring and matching? First, start mirroring and matching, or duplicating the words he, himself uses. The words that he uses in his conversation to you, are the ones he will receive favorably coming from you back to him. He doesn't want to hear unfamiliar words in a presentation. From now on, present your program or plan after listening to the words your prospect uses in his conversation to you and start mirroring and matching his words back to him.

Second, notice the tonality of the prospect's voice. If he speaks softly, I want you to speak softly. If he speaks loudly, you speak loudly. Speak slowly if he speaks slowly, or fast if he speaks fast. The way he talks to you, is the way he talks to himself. It is the way he best receives information from other people. If you can communicate to him the way he communicates to himself, you are on your way to getting your message through more favorably. From now on watch the tonality, tempo, speed, and the colloquialisms that prospects use in speech to you and mirror and match it back to them.

The third thing that I want you to mirror and match is the physiology of their bodies. Their hand and body movements, gestures, and mannerisms. If they sit up in the chair straight with their back against the chair, you do exactly the same. Sit the way they sit. If they sit more relaxed with their feet out in front of them, you do the same. If they tilt their head to one side, you tilt your head to one side. I want people to see something in you that reminds them unconsciously of themselves.

"There is something
about this person that I like,
why don't I try it?"

If you can accomplish this, their decision maker, or their subconscious mind, will say to themselves, you know there is something about this individual that I like. Why is that? Because they see something in you, that reminds them of themselves and they like themselves, so they will like you. Again, show me someone that likes you, and I'll show you an extremely high closing ratio.

I've been asked many times in making this presentation to groups, "Jack, does the possibility exist that the people might think that you are mimicking them?" My answer is always the same. I've been doing this for twenty years in my selling career and not once during that time has a person come up and said to me, "Jack are you mimicking me?" Everyone is looking for a friend. Everyone is looking for someone who is similar to them. Everyone is trying to find an individual they can be comfortable with, and, if you can make that person comfortable with you, you are on your way to having that person join your organization, or buying your product. That's what *rapport* is all about. You've seen salespeople or people in multi-level programs who have been extremely successful, and you ask yourself, what in the world is the ingredient here that is making that person successful? They might not necessarily be educated or great speakers, not well versed, not have a good plan, but what they have is the ability to build rapport with people, allowing those people to be comfortable with them, and all at once the customer will say to themselves, "there is something about this person that I like, why don't I try it?"

One of the most valuable tools that I can give you

Have you noticed how
different things appear
to different people
in different ways?

in this entire book is the technique of *mirroring and matching* your prospects. In the three areas of communication, the *words* you choose in making your presentation more acceptable, the *tonality* in which you present it, and the *physiology* of your body being the same as the person across from you, is how you achieve *rapport.*

The second part of this chapter addresses the issue of communication and how well you communicate with other people so that they receive the information that you are trying to convey. The question that you have to ask yourself is, *are you communicating with people the way those people communicate with themselves?* Now, I'll address that a little bit more later, but I want you to think about this: *Have you noticed how different things appear to different people in different ways?* When I say different things, that can mean a presentation such as a sales presentation or a presentation of a plan. Why do some people receive your information favorably and others do not? Many times in presenting your plan, I'm sure you've said to yourself, you know I've made this presentation many times and sometimes it appears to be extremely effective and other times it doesn't. Why is that? The presentation may very well sound and appear to be exactly the same every time to you. Why is it more effective on some people then others? Because *people receive information differently,* or in other words, they bring information into their decision maker, their mind, on different *channels.* You may very well be sending your information out on *your channel* and in fact they may receive it *on that channel because they have a similar channel as yourself,* but other times you may be

That one dominate sense is the
way you bring in most of your
information from the outside to
your decision maker.

sending it out on your channel and they are totally tuned into *another* channel. Again, *all people receive information differently.*

Let me give you a familiar example. On the freeway or expressway there is an automobile accident. Two cars come together and ten witnesses saw the accident. Now, the policeman comes and asks each witness what happened. He goes back to his car, sits down and reads their reports. They are all different! He goes back to the ten people and says, "Help me. Did you all see the same accident?" The answer is yes, they saw the same accident, but they brought the information about that accident into their minds differently. Why is that? Because people receive information differently. For possibly the first time you're going to understand why sometimes you are successful in presenting your plan or selling a product and sometimes you are not.

All human beings are born with five senses, unless one of them is impaired. The five senses are: *sight, hearing, touch, taste* and *smell.* Of those five senses three of them appear to dominate in our lives. In all people, *three* of your personal senses are stronger than the other two, and of those three stronger senses, one of them *predominates* or is the strongest sense you have. Consequently that one *dominate sense* is the way you bring in most of your information from the outside to your decision maker. Your mind. As networkers or salespeople, we have to identify that one dominate sense in each individual that we are talking to, and then appeal to that dominate sense. *We need to communicate through that one dominate sense.* The

If they don't see it, they don't believe it.

three dominate senses are visual or seeing; auditory or hearing; and kinesthetic or feeling. These are the three dominate senses in all human beings. If you were to take a mental inventory of yourself, of your three dominate senses, which one predominates? Is it the visual, auditory or kinesthetic? That is the channel that you use to bring information to your decision maker, your mind. Once you understand that, you can fully understand why some people receive information from you favorably and others don't.

Let's understand the *visual* person. Generally speaking, they are an active type of individual. Many times they are loud, demonstrative, quick voiced, and colorful. They keep their posture very erect, always seeing, picturing, and many times identifying themselves by the very clothes they are wearing, or jewelry that they compliment themselves with. They bring information in through their eyes. *If they don't see it, they don't believe it.* If you have an individual like this you're trying to sponsor into your network or sell a product to, he wants to *see* the program, results, and how it's going to benefit him. Such people have to bring in information though their eyes. Some of you are trying to talk to these people and explain your program to them, or sell them a product and they don't really hear anything you say. This type of individual, as you become more familiar with them, really are not great listeners. I'm not saying they don't hear anything you say, but they are not going to make a decision on what you are trying to convey to them based on what they hear. They are going to hake a decision based on what they *see,* and if it looks good, they will go for it and they'll buy it. If it doesn't look good, they won't.

If it sounds good, they'll buy it.

Therefore, if you're going to draw your plan out, you had better be explicit and artful in drawing the circles. If it's a product you are presenting to them, get that product out where they can see it. Let them see the results, look at the label, and have them hold it in their hands. These people make a decision based on almost 85% of what they see. If it doesn't look good, truthful, credible and appear to be everything that you are saying it is, there will be no sale.

The second type is the *auditory person.* This type brings in information through their *ears* and form a mental picture in their mind based on how your presentation *sounds* to them. Does that mean that they don't see you? No. They see you. They see your presentation or product. However they are not going to make a determining decision based on what they see. They're going to make a decision based on what they *hear.* If it sounds good, they'll buy it. If it doesn't sound good, no matter how it looks, they will not buy it. This type of individual's voice is a little bit softer or subdued. Their posture is relaxed. They move more slowly than the visual person. They don't carry themselves quite as erect. They are always listening, trying to hear. In fact, as you address them, they may very well have their eyes cast downward. I've heard many people say, "You know I just didn't get across to that individual. He wouldn't even look me in the eyes." You need to understand that these people don't want to look you in the eye. Not that they're trying to avoid you, but they're trying to concentrate on what you're saying. They don't want to be distracted by what they see. They want to put their full attention on what they're *hearing,* because they're going to make a deci-

If it feels good to them,
you've got a sale.

sion based on what they hear. If it sounds good, you have a sale or a new client. If it doesn't sound good, you have no sale. Therefore, you have to be a great story teller (a truthful story teller) but your story or presentation must have a beginning, middle, and end. When you get done with your story, it must sound so good to your prospect, that they can paint a picture mentally in their mind, based on your words, and how your proposal is going to benefit them and impact their lives. In fact, they are going to make a decision almost solely based on what they hear.

The third type of individual is the *kinesthetic* or the *feeling* type of person. This individual certainly sees you and hears what you're saying, but they are ingesting and digesting the information that you are bringing to them by how it makes them *feel*. If it feels good to them, you've got a sale. If it doesn't, then you don't. It may look fine, sound fine, but if they don't get a good feeling about it, no sale and no client. This individual is the most common. Statistics show that as many as 60 percent of people are what we call the *kinesthetic individual.* You can easily recognize this type of person. They are much quieter, have a more relaxed posture, are slower moving, speaks softly, and are reserved. Yes, this person listens to you and looks at you, but they are digesting the information based on what's coming out of their soul and from their heart. You might ask yourself: Is this truly the way people communicate with themselves? The answer is yes. Everyone communicates with themselves differently. It's like being on another channel and unless you tune into *their* channel, you're not going to reach them in a positive fashion. They will not nod their head yes

"You know, I just don't see
what you're saying."

Communicate with them on
their channel.

when you ask them for the order or to sign the application form.

Everyone that you come into contact with receives your information, such as a sales or a plan presentation, on different channels or wave lengths. Many times you have said to your best friend or spouse, "I don't think you heard a word I said." You are probably correct. Because if he is not an auditory or a listening person, he might very well be a *visual* or *kinesthetic* person. You've also heard the phrase, "you know, I just don't *see what you're saying.*" Visual people have to visualize what you are saying. They have to put those pictures in their mind, based on what they see. Auditory people have to put the picture in their mind on the benefits and advantages of your program or plan based on what they *hear.* Kinesthetic people have to paint the picture in their mind based on what they *feel.* If it doesn't feel right for this kind of person, you have no sale. Once you understand that everyone does not, and will not receive your information the same way, you are on your way to enhancing your closing ratio. That's why some people are so successful in building their network, because they can read people more quickly and communicate with them on their channel. How do you go about identifying these types of people quickly? It's not easy, but it is possible with just a little bit of practice. First, I would suggest figuring out what you are. Are you *visual, auditory* or *kinesthetic?* There's a great advantage in knowing what you are, because all at once you can use that as a bench mark to judge what other people are. The quickest way I found is to simply start asking a few questions, the who, what, where, when, and why

> **If I like you, I will probably be more apt to buy or be sponsored by you.**

questions. Draw your clients into conversation and observe their posture, voice tones, body movements, and eyes while listening, watching, and feeling where they are coming from. Then you can identify what their channel is. The minute you do that, you can pattern your presentation using your new information.

Two fine books on this subject exist that I recommend. The first book is by Michael Brooks and is called *Instant Rapport*. In it he gives a detailed and thorough description of how to identify different types of people. The second book I would recommend is by Anthony Robbins and is called *Unlimited Power*. Both of these authors are well respected and have researched this material in great length. It would be to your advantage to obtain these books.

In closing, I would like for you to remember that the quality of your life and the quality of your future networking career is going to be based on the quality of your communication with yourself and with other people. The challenge is to communicate with other people the way those people communicate with themselves. Remember, "the more you are like me, the more I will like you, and if I like you, I will probably be more apt to buy or be sponsored by you."

No one ingredient will make us successful.

Make the time.

Chapter Four
Time and Self-management

By the time you have reached this chapter, I'm sure you have come to realize that there is no one secret to success. So many times in life, people look outwardly to find success and in reality the only way to success is through ourselves. We have to become better people and fortify ourselves with all the tools and knowledge that, first, encourage success to come to us and, second, manage success once it becomes part of us. There is nothing magical and no one ingredient that will make anyone successful.

I once had a lady come up to me at one of my workshops and say, "Jack, I'm having a little problem here. I just don't know where I'm going to *find the time* to do some of the things that you're addressing here." I said you're absolutely correct. You're never going to *find the time* if you truly want success to come into your life, you're going to have to *make the time.* She said, "I'm not sure I understand, Jack."

Let's understand something here. Did God give everyone the same amount of time everyday? When we wake up in the morning do we have 24 hours to spend that day? We have to pick and choose how we are going to spend that time. So many people who are

Steal time from other
non-productive areas
of your life.

Turn the television off and turn
your life on.

not successful or who are constantly pursuing success do not spend their time to their best advantage. Therefore, why should they expect success to come into their lives? If they're truly going to be successful, they must take or steal time from other nonproductive areas of their lives, then apply it to the productive areas. This is what Chapter Four is about—how to best use your time.Time must become your greatest asset, or it will become your worst adversary. The first area where you might look to steal some time is the television set. How much time a week do you spend watching television? Interestingly enough, a recent survey in the newspaper said the average American family spends between forty and seventy hours per week watching television. Have you ever made any money watching television? Wouldn't it be to your advantage to turn the television off, and use that time to do some of the things that we discussed in Chapters One, Two, and Three? We waste so much of our life watching and doing nonproductive things. Television is one of the greatest stealers of our time and success. You might think about going down to the hardware store and getting yourself some duct tape. Put a little piece over the off/on knob. Turn the television *off* and turn your life *on*. You are never going to be a success by spending your time in front of the television. Another time stealer is our own families. We all want to be good parents, contribute and enjoy our families. However, how much time do we spend in such nonproductive areas such as running errands, driving our children back and forth to school, ball games, dances, and going here and there. We have to delegate some of those jobs and errands. In many cases, we could tell our children,

God gave each and everyone
of us the same 24 hours.

The magic word, no!

Delegate those types of jobs.

why don't you carpool to the ballgame or dance? You have to take charge of that time. I learned a long time ago that if you don't take charge of your life and your time, someone else will. Sadly, many times it's our own loved ones who take charge of our time. You've all heard that it's not the quantity of time you spend with your family, but the quality that's important. If we cut out all the unnecessary time wasters in our lives, it would free up more quality time for our families, and also allow us to devote more time to our business and career.

God gave each and everyone of us the same 24 hours. He didn't give my time to someone else to regulate and use; He gave it to me. If you truly want success you have to ask yourself, how badly do I want it? If you want it badly enough, you will learn to say the magic word: *no!* Do something today to better your own and your family's life. Time and self-management is one of the critical areas that we all fall down in.

Learn to delegate. Start delegating some things in your life that are nonproductive for you. You ask, "delegate? Who do I have to delegate to?" Do you still cut your grass at home? How long does it take you to cut your lawn? What would it cost to have a person come in to maintain it? Maybe $5 or $6 per hour? You might even enjoy cutting your own lawn, but there alone is two hours per week that you could better use. Is your time not worth more than $5 or $6 an hour, so that you could be paying someone else to do this type of work, so that you could build your career for yourself and your family? Delegate jobs like cutting grass, or washing your car. For example, if you made $25,000 per

Make a to do list.

It's like sending a message to
your godlike power.

year, each hour of your time is worth approximately $12 to $13 per hour to you. Wouldn't you be better served using that time to build your career? There are certain things in life that you have to turn over to other people and *pay* to have it done. Time becomes so important and precious, but we waste so much of it in nonproductive areas. We only have so many units of energy to spend during the week and if we want to spend some of those units to build our network marketing program, how in the world can we do it, if we are too tired from doing chores that could be delegated for just a few dollars per hour? Use the time you are taking from the other, nonproductive areas and put it to your advantage; delegate some jobs. We've got plenty of time if we properly use it to our best advantage.

Next, each day make a *to do* list of what you want to accomplish. Put down everything that you want to accomplish that day, whatever that might be. Then, prioritize your list. What are the most important things that you want to accomplish? Put them in an order of priority and start working on your list. The amazing thing is, once you affirm some of these things in writing, it's like sending a message to your godlike power, your subconscious mind, to get it done. Write things down. Everyday make yourself a new list. In the evening review the list. See what you have accomplished and check them off as you go, giving yourself a pat on the back for all you have accomplished. The ones that you haven't accomplished carry over to the next day and make them a priority for the new day.

Next, organize your desk or the work area that you have dedicated to network marketing. Organize your

A cluttered desk indicates a
cluttered mind.

Getting quiet and
within yourself.

work, and file your information, doing everything in a logical, orderly fashion so that you don't have to spend a lot of time searching for or trying to find things. I've seen people trying to work at a cluttered desk. *A cluttered desk indicates a cluttered mind.* Keep your mind and desk organized. You cannot believe the amount of time you'll save just by keeping things in a structured manner. We waste so much of our time searching, looking, and seeking information that we're trying to give to someone else. Many times we get frustrated that we can't find it. Always keep yourself organized, whether it's your car, desk, home, or office.

Another area that you must look into is getting yourself quiet sometime during each day. You've read and heard many examples of people sitting in a meditative, quiet or a prayer like state. Sometimes when you are quiet and close your eyes and try not to think of anything, cleansing your mind of everything that's going on in your life, great ideas will come to you. By getting quiet and within yourself and not trying to think of anything, you will be amazed at some of the great ideas that come into your mind and consciousness.

Another important idea is to structure the phone calls that you receive during the day. Learn how to control your end of the phone calls that you receive. So many times we receive phone calls from people just wasting time, calling just to chitchat. They're wasting your time too! Learn how to control the conversation and try to bring your phone calls to a head by finding out their purpose, and then going from there to ending the call. Don't waste your time on the phone.

When do you do your best work?

Truly successful people are always on time for appointments or engagements, whether in sponsoring or selling. Make it a point the rest of your life, that if you tell someone you'll be there at a specific time, you're there at that time. Many times being late to an appointment only means that you have not disciplined yourself enough to get yourself there on time. From the other people's perspective, by keeping them waiting you're telling them that you don't respect their time. Being on time is extremely important to success, but it's also just as important for building a reputation of integrity.

Every person has certain times of their day when they are more creative and productive. Some people are morning people and others are evening people. A good idea would be to sit down and try to analyze yourself to see where your high level of energy is. When do you do your best work? Is it in the morning or in the evening? You must know when the most productive time of your day is and start channeling your efforts into that time frame. Your time frame may only be two, three, or four hours at a certain time of the day. But, you need to realize that you can get more done in that time frame because your energy level, enthusiasm, and motivation is higher. Everything about you is better if you work within that particular time frame. So figure out when you are at your best level of energy, then dedicate that time toward your network marketing plan. Everyone has that inner metabolism, but it's different for different people. Work at your peak energy level and you will accomplish more in that time than you will at any other time of your day.

Get it done, achieve a good result and go on to do something else.

Watch your minutes and the hours will take care of themselves.

One of the greatest keys to success is time, how you manage it and how you manage yourself. You've seen people who seem to be running helter skelter through life and they never seem to be getting anything done. You've seen other people methodically approach a project, work through it, use their time, get it done with good results, and go on to something else. Those people accomplish more in life than anyone else. Why not get organized? If we are to be successful, we have to look at our time as something precious, because once the day is spent, it's spent and we can't do it over. Use your time to your best advantage and make every minute count. Watch your *minutes* and the *hours* will take care of themselves.

Finally, when you are away from work and your organizational goals, release your career thoughts. Cleanse your mind. Let your mind replenish and refresh itself. Do not carry your work with you into all aspects of your life, because you will bog yourself down and it will actually mentally drown you. So, when you're not out working or building your organization, release your thoughts and let them go. But, when you get back into that right time frame, kick it into high gear.

Time is one of our strongest assets when we use it correctly. It also can become one of our worst adversaries, if we let it slip away.

"Imagination rules the world".

Chapter Five
Imagination

In the early 1800s a Frenchman by the name of Napoleon Bonaparte made the statement "imagination rules the world." Here was a man in his late-twenties who not only became emperor of France, but also conquered most of western Europe. He didn't do it with vast armies or superb weaponry. He did it with magnificent battle plans. Even today, military strategists study some of Napoleon's battle concepts and ideas. He always imagined new ways to approach and conquer his enemy and created battle plans that had not been thought of before.

If imagination ruled the world in the early 1800s, do you suppose it still rules the world now? Absolutely yes! Look at what has happened in our lifetime as far as technology, computerization, new inventions and space technology. Where did all this come from? It came from someone's imagination. Do you suppose we should adapt some of those same imaginative ideas in network building? Yes. The problem is that, in many cases, we have been stymied or discouraged from using our imagination in parts of our lives. Do you realize that from the time we started to school when we were five or six years old possibly until we

Innovative, creative
producing human beings.

went into the military or college, our imagination was oppressed or discouraged from being used. We were regimented and even programmed. You do this. Do that. March this way. Stand that way. Go to class. Every part of our whole life was orchestrated for us, which stopped us from using our imagination. Why did the school and military systems do this? Because it made us easier to organize, structure, discipline, and manage. If everyone is doing the same thing, at the same time, it makes the job of the people in charge much easier. So, here's the problem. We get out of the military or college and we don't know how to manage our own lives; we don't know how to make a living. School really does not prepare us properly to be innovative, creative, producing human beings. We have forgotten how to think and even how to use our own imaginations.

As an example, readers who are over fifty years old, think back to when you were young. Think of how you entertained yourself. There was only radio then because television had not been commercially produced yet. Maybe you had a neighborhood theater that you got to attend once a week. Remember how you used to entertain yourselves in the evenings? Remember the different types of games or activities that you and your friends organized? Do you remember sitting down in the evening after dark and listening to the radio with your parents and how your mind ran rampant? Your imagination almost overwhelmed you with what you heard on the radio, and in your mind you could really see what was being described on that radio. Think how you felt when you listened to some of the programs like "Fiber McGee and Molly." When Fiber McGee opened that closet door, all that para-

Remember when you were
a youngster.

Peoples' futures were started in
their early years by using their
imagination.

phernalia fell out, and you heard all the funny noises, you could envision and see it with your own mind. It was almost like you were there. That's *imagination*. Think about how as a youngster, you listened to some of the serials that were on the radio such as "Captain Midnight," "Terry and the Pirates," "The Lone Ranger and Tonto" and "Captain Marvel." Think about some of fight scenes you heard on the radio. You could see the villain getting beaten up. You could hear the sounds of the fight and through your mind you were really there. That's *imagination*. How about when you played baseball or any other sport? Today youngsters have organized league play. They have uniforms, beautiful ball diamonds to play on, and uniformed umpires to officiate. But remember when you were a youngster and you had to make up your own pick up games. No uniforms, no baseball spikes, no umpires, most of the time not enough players to get a full game going. So you made your own rules and played baseball by the hour. And of course, you were always a Ted Williams, Stan Musial or a Joe Dimaggio when you got up to the plate. Even then you tried to be like that successful person.

Today, I wonder if youngsters could even organize or have the imagination to orchestrate their own games. Someone else would probably have to do it for them. Back when we were young, at night we used our imaginations and played hide-and-seek or kick the can. You used your imagination to consider the possibilities and determine how to outwit your opponent. Many times peoples' futures were started in their early years by using their *imagination*. They could see what they wanted to be when they became an adult.

Ingenious and inventive way to earn the money.

Young people need to use and rediscover their imagination.

Today, the first thing that young people do when they come in from school, is turn on the television set regardless of what's on. They just turn it on. Most of the time they are either watching, half watching, or waiting for someone to come home to take them to some organized activity. It appears that they have lost the ability to entertain themselves. They want to watch someone else perform on television or on the playing field rather than participate themselves.

Let me give you another example. Go back again to when we were young and wanted to raise a little money to go to the movie house or possibly to buy something special that we wanted. Money, in most cases, if you were like me, was not readily available from our parents. Therefore, you had to come up with some ingenious and inventive way to *earn* the money. Think about all the things you did when you were young to earn extra money. Maybe you collected soda bottles, washing them out and taking them back to the store for the two cent refund. Maybe you cut grass, raked leaves, or worked in the neighbor's garden. Maybe you shoveled snow, ran errands for a neighbor or went to the grocery store. If you're over fifty, you might have gone down to the ice house to get a block of ice for the little lady across the street. The fact was, you had to *earn* your money, and to do that you had to use your *imagination.* Things just weren't handed to you so easily. You don't want to go back to that time, and I assure you I don't either. You may also say that you want your children to have things better than you did and I do too. But, we as grown ups and parents must instill this desire to use and rediscover their imagination in our young people. I believe our educa-

The opposite of conformity is
courage.

Changing is one of the most
difficult and challenging things
we can do.

tion system is also at fault to some degree. I've seen students who don't know their multiplication tables, and don't know how to add, subtract, and divide, because it's easier to do with a calculator, and I've known teachers who agree. But, if you don't learn to do those things for yourself, in your own mind, what happens if your calculator batteries go dead? You won't even be able to tell time by looking at the manual clock, because you need a digital one. We know the computer programs in school, in most cases, are good, but also in many cases they stymie a young person's imagination. Now they put things into a computer, and it comes out with all different types of answers or options, instead of doing it themselves with their imaginations.

What if we said that from this day forward, that we were no longer going to conform? Not only are we not going to conform, but we are going to start being totally independent thinkers. We are going to start turning our imagination loose. I don't mean being a rebel, breaking the law, or being a renegade. I mean being a creative, innovative human being from this day forward. My brother, Bill, and I have always said that the opposite of conformity is courage. It certainly takes courage on our part not to conform. It takes courage because when someone is different, it sets them apart from most. Every time we try to do something different that means we have to change. Changing is one of the most difficult and challenging things we can do. However, if we are truly going to be successful in our networking program, we must become more innovative, creative, and imaginative people. Now you might ask yourself, "how do I stir up and recreate this imagi-

Literally drown yourself with
those tapes.

Reawaken this magical giant
within you.

native ability within myself?" But first you should ask yourself what tools you have at your disposal, or that you could become reacquainted with, that would help stir up this magical giant? Do you realize that we, as human beings, are the only species on this earth with this creative, innovative, and imaginative quality? However, in our early lives, we have been trained not to use it.

Let's talk about some of the tools that we can use to recreate our imagination. How about cassette tapes? Correct me if i'm wrong, but don't you always feel better and get some really great ideas after listening to a good tape by a good motivational or human development speaker? Find yourself some tapes that you like and continually listen to them. I mentioned in a previous chapter to find one or two tapes that strike your fancy or hits your chord then literally drown yourself with those tapes. Listen to them over and over again. Every time you listen to them you will hear something new and get some new ideas. Why? Because every time you listen to them, you are a new and different person than you were just a few moments before. The cassette tape is an excellent tool to reestablish this imaginative quality we all have within us. I can document many cases where tapes have actually changed peoples lives. The tapes get these creative juices going again and reawaken this magical giant within you.

The second tool you might think about is your network marketing meeting. Instead of the usual meeting, why not think of new and innovative ideas to use and introduce at your meetings? Instead of having basically the same meeting time after time, why not have new,

In a mastermind group there is
no such word as can't.

inspirational ones each time? How about a mastermind group? Find some different types of people from various careers. Get them all together and get some synergism going. Getting together thus enables each of you to grow your own business. Find people who are good thinkers. Get together in a group atmosphere and start exploring. Remember, in a mastermind group there is no such word as can't. When you get into a mastermind group really "blue sky it" and the possibilities and results will be great. Let's define a mastermind group and see if I can paint a picture of how it can benefit you. First, organize and find yourself four, six, or eight other people. They must be high thinking individuals. They can, but don't necessarily have to be, in the network marketing business. You might have a banker, a real estate agent, and a business or entrepreneur type person. Get some people who have different reference points and thoughts that are dissimilar from your own. Meet in one of your homes once a month to explore and imagine how you can help each other with new ideas or with problems any of you might be having in business.

Another way to stimulate your imagination is through books. I don't mean love novels. I mean good human development, business, creative, and motivational books. A lot of good authors are willing to share their ideas. Everyone reading this book should have one or two other books going at the same time. Find yourself some books that you like. If you need a good example, look at some of Richard Bach's books. Richard Bach uses such imagination that he is really stimulating and motivating in his books. Earl Nightingale, Norman Vincent Peale, and Wayne Dyer

We have to fly more with
our mind.

Find yourself a good book.

Become a great listener.

are other great authors. Wayne Dyer is a person of great consciousness. He has a book out called *The Gift From Eykus*. When you read this book, you have to use your imagination. The same with Richard Bach. When he starts talking in his book on *Illusions*, all at once your mind starts clicking in some thoughts and starts flying. We have to fly more with our mind. We have to get our creative thinking going. Books are a great way to do this. We do not read enough. We read, but most of it is junk reading. They have no brain stimulation to them. In fact, all those gossip column magazines are negative reading. Don't get involved in that type of reading. Find yourself a good book. Have one on your nightstand, your breakfast table, and one in your living room. Have these books available and keep them going. Books are a great way to stimulate your imagination.

Another way you might learn new things and have new thoughts is in conversation with two or more people. I found that I can learn a whole lot more by listening. When you get into a conversation, don't try to dominate it. Try to ask people questions. I always ask people questions with the six magical words that we spoke of before; the who, what, where, when, why, and how. Get that other person talking, and then listen. You never know when an idea or good thought is going to come to mind. Become a great listener. So many times I've seen people trying to dominate conversations. You'll be better served turning yourself into a great listener.

The journey to success is simpler than most people realize. In many cases, people say to themselves, "It

There's nothing magical about
success.

It's a process of self
development.

appears to be such a difficult task, I don't even think I'll start." Here again, I'll say it's not such a difficult task. You just have to start, taking one step at a time. It's all obtainable. There's nothing magical about success and achieving goals and dreams. It's a process of self development of ourselves. It's a process of being the best human being, salesperson, and networker that we are capable of becoming. We all have it within our grasp, but many times we shortchange ourselves, because of a lack of imagination.

> # Goal setting is one of the key factors that will ensure your success.

Chapter 6
The Power of Goal Setting

I believe that *goal setting* is a key factor in ensuring success in your business, physical and spiritual well-being, and in all life's endeavors. In a study that was conducted over the course of twenty years, involving a graduating class at a prestigious northeastern university. One hundred graduating students were interviewed and asked if they had actually sat down and written out some goals for their lives. Out of the 100 graduating students, only four had actually sat down and written out their goals. Twenty years later, those same 100 students were interviewed about their lives since their graduation. Here's the enlightening results of that study. The four percent that had said they had sat down and written out some goals seemed to have a very happy outlook on life. They appeared to have a great family structure and enjoyed a good quality of health. They also seemed to have a real spiritual meaning in their lives. And most importantly those four percent, four people out of the 100 original graduating class, were worth more money than the remaining ninety-six students combined. Four people out of 100 were actually worth more, achieved more, and acquired more than the remaining ninety-six. Now how could that be true? How does that happen? You

There truly is real power
in setting some goals.

see, I believe there truly is real power in setting some goals. You may ask what power? What generates the power? What makes it happen? To explain this we must go back to some of the great spiritual and human developers of the past and discuss their beliefs. Many of their ideas you may have heard or read before, and maybe it didn't register at the time. The first teacher is one of my mentors, a man that I respect, have read and have listened to his audio cassette tapes for many years. I believe Earl Nightingale helped more people become successful than any other human developer. Earl recently passed away, but not before becoming one of the greatest men that ever lived as far as trying to help people reach their full potential. Many years ago, he recorded an audio tape called the "Strangest Secret." On that tape he taught what many religious teachers have said in the past, but with a different style of saying it. Earl's secret was really not a secret, but something that has been said for thousands of years— You become what you think about. If you think about success, you will have success. If you think about failure, you will have failure. If you think about health, happiness, and prosperity, you will have health, happiness, and prosperity. If you think about love, caring and empathy, that's what you are going to have; however, if you let your thoughts be negative then those are the thoughts that will be manifested into your life. Earl believed as I do, that you create what you think about. An even greater teacher 2,000 years ago said it in another way. He said, "As man thinketh in his heart, so shall he be." Many people thought he was just talking about love, care, and religious beliefs. I believe Christ was saying that, whatever you think with your

"The body will manifest what
the mind harbors."

"As man thinketh in his heart,
so shall he be."

mind and heart in a dominant fashion, that's what will be manifested into your life. That's why he said keep your thoughts good. Be careful about what you pray for because what you pray for will come into your life. Christ said it, Earl Nightingale said it, and still another mentor of mine also said it. I have great respect for Dr. Denis Waitley. I have read about and listened to his audio cassettes many times and he has had a very positive influence on my life. Denis said, "The body will manifest what the mind harbors." Is he also saying the same thing with just different words as Earl Nightingale or Jesus Christ? Yes! All the learned or great people are saying the same thing. Sometimes we just have to hear it from different people coming from different directions. When we set some goals they become part of our dominant thoughts. When they become dominant thoughts they *have* to be manifested into our lives. That's the law. That's not man's law, but I believe that's God's law. We will manifest our current dominant thoughts into our lives. Start practicing to be the best human being that you possibly can, by having the best possible thoughts in your mind. This is our task. This is our life's goal.

The Benefits of Goal Setting

You might be asking yourself, "Do I really have to set some goals to be successful? Do I really have to set some goals to make these wonderful things manifest in my life?" The answer is yes! "Are there truly benefits and what are they, so that I can better motivate myself to achieve these goals?" There certainly are benefits, because goal setting improves self-image. When you have something to work towards then you stand for

You cannot outdistance your
own self-image.

You can start visualizing.

something. You are not on the picket fence of life. You have an objective to accomplish, and in that journey your self-image is greatly enhanced. I've said this before, but it bears repeating. *You cannot outdistance your own self-image.* You enhance your self-image when you set some goals. In fact, it improves you today and continuously makes you better for all the tomorrows. Goal setting also gives you the confidence to allow you to build and fortify from within to make you a stronger person.

Setting goals also lowers your frustration level. Many times we get little road blocks in life and get off the path to success. With goals to work on, you are not going to let that happen to you. You are going to have a course, structure, and direction in your life. The little hiccups that come along eventually become less and less significant. You can now take less notice of them, because you have something that has a bigger purpose. Goal setting helps you to visualize what you truly want in life. Most people live their lives in such a haphazard fashion and then wonder why they get poor results. By having goals you can start visualizing what you want to actuate in your life. When you visualize, you know where to take action and what to work on. You know what direction to take. So by visualizing, you take action and by taking action, you start manifesting or actualizing all those things that you want to occur in your life. Goal setting forces you to set priorities. It gives you the proper direction for your pursuits. It forces you to be specific. That's one of the great benefits of goal setting. It does not allow you to go off on tangents that are not going to enhance your life. Goal setting also defines reality and sets it apart

It's no longer wishful thinking.

Pro-active instead of re-active.

from wishful thinking. You now have some concrete things you want to work on. It's no longer daydreaming. It's no longer wishful thinking. It's what you want to happen or what you want to acquire in your life.

Another great benefit to setting goals is that it serves as a criterion for sharpening your decision making. It defines what is important as well as what is not. So many times we make decisions based on immediate pressures. For example, we make short-term decisions based on a car or house payment that needs to be paid, instead of basing our decisions on the long term. Goal setting makes us more pro-active instead of re-active in our journey through life. Last, but not least, I think human beings are the most motivated when they have a commitment, job, task, or goal to strive for. It's difficult to motivate ourselves when we have nothing to look forward to. We human beings are a goal striving mechanism; we need something to work towards, so that we don't go through life aimlessly and without purpose.

If according to successful people one of the key elements to success is setting some goals for your life, then why don' more people do it? I've identified some possible reasons. See if any of these are more or less the same excuses that you have been using on yourself.

1. *Setting goals makes people accountable to themselves and others.* Many people don't want to be held accountable nor to push themselves to be successful. They are satisfied to take what comes along. People search out and secure a job based not on what they want to do with their lives, but on how much money it will bring in. Isn't it a shame that so

They really have no plan to
achieve the goals.

many people in this country get a job *only* to earn income regardless of how enjoyable that job or task may be.

2. *People fear that they may have to give up something that at that point in their life seems important to them.* In other words, if you set some goals, you're going to have to have a plan to achieve those goals. And, in the exercise of that plan, you're going to have to give up some things that you presently have been doing. People will say to themselves, "Yes, I'd like to acquire that particular goal or I'd like to achieve this objective, but I'd have to give up watching television, or going to ball games," or some other activity that they enjoy. They don't want to give up something even though it is far less significant and important to their well-being.

3. The third reason why I believe people don't set goals, *they really have no plan to achieve the goals.* Furthermore, I believe they are afraid to start because they have no concept on how to accomplish any goals they do set. Many times they do fall into the category of daydreaming or wishful thinking. They say they would like to have a particular goal, but that they have no way to acquire it, and because they have no plan for achieving their goals, they don't test themselves.

4. *They are afraid of failure.* People are afraid that if they put themselves on the spot and don't achieve their goals they are going to be ridiculed by others and shamed by themselves. Now, think about that for just a moment. They will say to themselves, "I don't know if I should set that goal because if I fail

If they fail to make a decision,
then that, in itself, is a decision.

to achieve it, how am I going to face myself and other people?" It's better to achieve only one step of a goal than never to attempt it at all.

5. *In the process of executing the plan to a goal, they realize that certain things are going to have to be given up and certain people may not be pleased, particularly family members or close personal friends.* You have to dedicate some time to your plan that you previously had with other people doing other activities. You may be afraid of disappointing some people, possibly even your own family. I think this is a big, big reason why many people don't set goals. They are letting other people control their lives.

6. *It takes a decision.* It forces you to sit down and make a decision regarding what you are going to do with your life. Many people have a difficult time making this type of decision or commitment, even if it's for the betterment of themselves and their future. People should realize that if they fail to make a decision, then that, in itself, is a decision. You just made a decision to do nothing! That's an extremely important point to think about.

7. *People let others decide what is best for them.* We take other people's suggestions on where to live and work, what type of clothes to buy, what type of car to own, or what type of home we should live in. We let other people live our lives for us. Even though the suggestions, I'm sure, are well intended from family members and loved ones, we are letting other people decide for us what is best for us. Therefore, we just don't have to make any decisions to set any goals.

"Yes, I've got this dream.
I can achieve it."

If it is not important, you won't
achieve it.

8. *People have to be truthful with themselves.* You have to stop making excuses for your possible future failure. Instead of sitting there analyzing yourself and saying, "Yes, I've got this dream. I can achieve it. I can acquire it, if I dedicate myself to it, instead of self-doubting myself and saying I don't know if this is possible. No one in my family has ever accomplished this, why do I think I can?" Be truthful with yourself first. If you are not truthful with yourself, there is no way in the world you are ever going to have the success that you desire.

9. *People fail to set goals because it forces them, as an individual, to set priorities.* We have to prioritize our life. Many times people get up in the morning and just seem to take what comes along in the day. To accomplish your goals you have to set a plan to achieve them. You have to find out what's really important to you. The biggest criterion to achieving your goal is that it has to be important to you. If it is not important, you won't achieve it. Therefore, you must set some priorities. You must have a burning desire for what you want to do with your life in four areas: your career, family, spiritual beliefs, and physical well-being. You *must* set some priorities in these four areas. Goal setting forces you to do that. Goal setting forces you to start prioritizing things that are going to be important in your self development and in your future success.

10. *They just don't believe that they have the tenacity to stay with the course.* They believe that the very first time there is a hiccup or roadblock, they will give up and be a failure. Many people don't have

Don't judge or try to justify your desires.

the tenacity to stay the entire length of time it takes to set up and achieve a goal. They will say, "Yes, I tried goal setting last Tuesday and it didn't work." Well, you have to set a goal and a plan and then you must work at that plan. Many people may not have the ability to stay the course, but, more importantly, many don't *think* they have the ability.

Now that we know why most people don't set goals, I would suggest you take a mental inventory of yourself to see if any of these are stopping you from writing out your goals. If they are, then you now know where to start. Here's what I want you to do: Sit down by yourself and get comfortable and get a notebook or a legal pad. Start writing out what you want to happen in your life. As you write, don't judge or try to justify your desires. Now, it is extremely important you remember there are four areas of your life that must be covered. Your career or your multilevel marketing business, your family, spiritual growth, and your physical well-being. (We must learn to take better care of our physical body. In many cases, we take better care of our home, automobile, or adult toys than we do ourselves.) Now, as you sit down to write your goals, be very specific and say exactly what you want to accomplish. If there is a different pin or achievement level, write it down in the order that you want to achieve it. If there is a dollar volume that you want to reach, write that down. For example, earning $50,000 a year by January 1 of whatever year you're focusing on, or $100,000 a year, or whatever your figure is. Write it down and write it specifically. Do not judge whether you are capable, should have, or deserve any of the things you write down. Just write down what

These are your goals in life.

Goals are not promises to
yourself, but they are
commitments to yourself.

They ask little of life, and life
pays their price.

you want to happen in your business, family, spiritual beliefs, and physical well-being These are the areas that you need to acknowledge and grow yourself. Your physical well-being is important, because your body is going to take you on this journey. If there is some weight you want to lose, write it down. "I will lose twenty pounds by such and such a date," or "I will have myself in better physical condition. I will teach myself better eating habits." Write everything that you want to happen down on a piece of paper. Now remember, these are your goals; don't confide them to anyone else, even the ones closest to you. Let them do their own individual goals. These are *your* goals in life. Don't look for approval. Don't look for someone else's acceptance. You write down what you want to happen in your life. This is your life. This is your journey. Do not consult anyone else and remember, as you write your goals down, all at once you are starting to put a road map together on the things that you want to accomplish. It's a desire for progress, or future progress that you are going to have. Goals are not promises to yourself, but they are commitments to yourself. They are not wishes or daydreams; they are visions of what you want to happen in your life. After this is completed, sit back and take a breather. Congratulate yourself. You have done something that 96 percent of the people in this country never do. They ask little of life, and life pays their price. Few write goals down. You are one of the 4 percent that have actually written out their goals for life. After you write down your goals, start prioritizing them. There are going to be some goals that are extremely important to you, some short-term, medium-range and long-

You must build a plan.

Now it is critical to make a list
of the things that are
stopping you.

term goals. Start prioritizing your goals as far as their importance to you and what you want to achieve in life. Most people never do this, and then they wonder why they never achieve the success they desire. You have done it! You should congratulate yourself. It is a task well deserving of applause!

After you have prioritized your goals, you should have four lists: One for career, one for family, one for spiritual, and one for physical. It is one thing to list your goals, but they are not going to manifest themselves all alone. You must build a plan to accomplish them. Let's say that you want to get to the next pin level in your organization. What is it going to take to get you there or, more importantly, what personal improvements do you need to make to accomplish this? First, write the goal out in a positive manner. Example: I will be a (Title of that pin level) by January 1, 199X. It's important to list your exact goal and the time frame for accomplishing it. It is also extremely important to set a starting date. Now it is critical to make a list of the things that are stopping you from accomplishing your goal. What is keeping you from achieving this pin level? Be honest! Now is not the time to fool yourself. Remember the saying, *A problem identified, is a problem half solved.* The problem most people have in achieving and accomplishing their goals is a failure to acknowledge what it is that is stopping them from attaining it. Make yourself a list. For example:

1. I don't make appointments over the phone well. (shy, embarrassed, etc.)

2. I don't present the plan well. (knowledge of the plan, drawings etc.)

> # Ask your upline sponsor.
>
> # Start formulating a plan to correct these short comings.

3. I never have enough time. (procrastination, priorities, etc.)

4. My prospects seem nervous when I talk with them.
   (don't establish good communication, eye contact,
   etc.)

5. I never can answer all the prospects questions. (not
   attending enough product meetings and seminars to
   acquire adequate information)

6. I don't know enough about my products. (not
   spending enough time with products to learn all
   about them)

These are just some examples of what could be
stopping you. Yours may be different, but whatever
they are, write them down and acknowledge them. If
by chance, you don't know where you are weak, ask
your upline sponsor to help you identify them and be
big enough to accept his or her input. By writing
down your weak areas, you now know where to start
working to accomplish your goal. Again, a problem
identified is a problem half solved.

Start formulating a plan to correct these short comings.

1. Sit down and write out a script for making phone
   appointments. Practice with your script on an
   unplugged phone. Teach yourself to relax, speak
   clearly, and to the point. Don't make your script too
   long and remember you are giving them an opportunity to hear about something new and exciting.

2. Seek out knowledge about your business plan.
   Know it inside and out. Be able to anticipate any
   possible questions your prospect may have and

There is never not enough time
for your future success!

You may encounter some
roadblocks or obstacles along
the way. That's okay!

equip yourself with the answers. Practice your pre-sentation, so that it is smooth and to the point. Don't start repeating yourself. Practice your presentation in front of your family, or on a video camera so that you can replay and make corrections as needed.

3. If time, or lack of it, is your problem, study the time and self-management chapter in this book. Remember, there is never not enough time for your future success!

4. If people skills are not your forte, study the rapport chapter in this book and practice the techniques suggested.

5. Get involved with all your organization's functions; attend and take part in all the meetings. This will bring to you monumental knowledge, enabling you to share problems while keeping you motivated to go on to achieving your goals.

6. Weak product knowledge is easy to correct. Study the products until they become part of yourself, and you know them inside and out. Product sheets, videos, workshops, and spending time with the products will enable you to feel comfortable with them.

Now that you have a plan to correct what's wrong. It's not that difficult to start correcting your weak areas. *It's very important to remember that you may encounter some roadblocks or obstacles along the way.* That's okay! That's normal. Just don't quit! Stop, acknowledge what's happening, make some adjust-ments, and go on. If it were easy, everyone would do it! Remember, winners do what losers won't!

I believe God put everything inside of us when He created us.

It is not His job to come by our home in a catering truck to see what we need.

As you accomplish or achieve some of your objectives congratulate yourself! Reward yourself and your spouse by going out to dinner, or buy yourself a new tie or dress, whichever the case may be. It is important to acknowledge your accomplishments so that you feel energized to move on to the next project. Remember, we need to constantly work on ourselves to be the very best we can be.

I believe God put everything inside of us when He created us. It is now up to us to develop it, if we are going to enjoy all the happiness and prosperity He wants us to have. It is not His job to come by our home in a catering truck to see what we need. He's done His job beautifully and now it's up to us to grow ourselves into the very best human being possible. When we do that, success and all His abundance will be yours!

Let's review what you have accomplished by accepting and implementing the information in this chapter.

1. You now understand the importance of setting some goals. Without goals you have no idea where you will end up, and what you can hope to accomplish.

2. You are now aware of some of the reasons most people never undertake this task, and possibly you can relate and identify with some of the stated reasons.

3. You now have a workable plan or blueprint for writing out and acknowledging your own personal goals. And equally important, you know that there are four areas that must be covered to truly enjoy all the joy and success you desire.

4. You now have a way to identify what is or has been

Belief • Faith • Love

stopping you from achieving your goals, plus a method for correcting those shortcomings.

5. You also understand the importance of rewarding yourself after a goal is accomplished.

Do you realize how far you have come into building yourself into the type of individual, who not only attracts success, but also attracts other people to build the type of organization you desire?

However, you are not quite finished yet with this chapter. I challenge you to do something I learned from Earl Nightingale's cassette, "The Strangest Secret."

Note the goal card below:

"Ask, And It Shall Be Given You."

"Seek, And Ye Shall Find."   BACK SIDE

"Knock, and It Shall be Opened Unto You."

My Goal Is_____

I am an _____Distributor

Date: _____   FRONT SIDE

Signed:_____

Belief • Faith • Love

Make four of these cards on your typewriter or computer: one for each of the four areas we covered in the chapter. On each card, put your number 1 prioritized goal, dating, and signing it. As Earl stated on his

It's the law!

tape, and as l strongly recommend in this book, you should carry these cards with you at all times. Read and visualize them several times each day and right before you go to sleep at night. By practicing this habit, your goals are implanted into your mind and become your dominant thoughts. When they become your constant, dominant thoughts, they have to be manifested or actualized into your life. It's the law!

Attitude has to be at or near
the top of anyone's list.

Chapter Seven
Attitude and Concentration

One of my mentors, Dr. Denis Waitley, says in many of his great books and tapes that, in his opinion, attitude is the one key element to anyone's success. I certainly wouldn't disagree with him or say he is wrong. Even though other tangibles make up the total picture for success in this book, attitude has to be at or near the top of anyone's list.

Take myself as an example. I was a general manager of a maintenance chemical manufacturing plant in Dallas, Texas. I had been asked by the company president to move from my home in Michigan, where I had developed a very successful sales territory, to Texas, to build a satellite plant to manufacture, sell, and distribute our line of cleaning products. My new responsibilities would include operations, marketing, and sales of our product line. This was a great opportunity and challenge for me. My challenge, or problem if you will, is that I had no experience in hiring and training *manufacturing* people. I knew what to look for in a new prospective salesman, but I was a little uncertain what to look for in a potential manufacturing person. (Little did I know how similar they were.) I quickly found out to look for the *same* character traits, values,

Go ahead and make that
second call as quickly
as you can.

work history, and most important, attitude as I had found in potential salespeople in the past. I always found myself looking for this qualification in any person, above anything else. I knew that if an applicant had a great attitude, I could teach him or her anything about the plant operations. I really didn't concern myself with any experience applicants brought with them, because experience can actually prove detrimental, if it's developed with bad habits that have to be changed. That alone would present another challenge. So, attitude became my number one qualification for hiring new people. My theory was proven correct over and over in the years to come, by the fact that our Texas plant was the most profitable, most efficient, and fun place to work over all our other company operations. The attitude of our entire work force made this possible. Another illustration of how one's attitude plays a dynamic part in one's success was given to me personally by the president of the company I just described. Leonard L. Mednick was a man I greatly admired, respected, and enjoyed working for. In one of our personal times over dinner one night, he shared with me a piece of advice that he taught to his salespeople when he was the national sales manager of our company before becoming president. He told me, he always advised salesmen that in making their first sales call of the day, no matter what result had occurred in that call, good or bad, sale or no sale, go immediately to the next call with no hesitancy. He then explained to me the reason for this, which I have never forgotten and consider a valuable piece of information. Mr. Mednick said if your first sales call was a success and you left with a nice order, you always felt

You have to replace a
negative thought or action
with a positive one.

great and on top of the world and your attitude was at it's highest level. So, go ahead and make that second call as quickly as you can, and it will most likely turn out as well or, if not, even better than the first because of that great attitude. But what happens if the first one ended up to be a failure? Get right back out there and make that next sales call now! Why? Because you want to replace all those negative feelings and non-success attitude with a very positive one as quickly as possible. If you don't immediately act, then you may never replace the negative results. So get right back out there and make that sales call!

We all have heard that if you fall off a horse, get right back in the saddle again. Don't let the experience of falling off the first time stop you from trying it the second time. If you wait, you're liable not to get back on that horse ever again. It's no different than when young parents stop their baby from getting up and try-ing again after the child has fallen while learning to walk. All parents continue to encourage their young child to get up and try again, even if the child gets hurt a little in that first fall. It's no different for you in build-ing your business. If you get rejected on your first try, your fifth try, or your one hundredth try—pick your-self up, get out, and show your plan again. The whole key in these experiences is that you have to replace a negative thought or action with a positive one. Teach yourself to control your attitude!

A final point to remember before we go on: *Your attitude controls your actions,* and, I might add, your actions control your results.

Attitude can affect your business. Janet and I had

Your attitude controls your
actions. Your actions
control your results.

an encounter on a recent holiday weekend that illustrates my point. We had decided at the last minute to spend the weekend in Jefferson, Texas, an old historic town about three hours east of Dallas. It is one of our favorite spots to go to, because of its history and the fact that the town and many of it's homes have been kept and restored to their original condition. It's a beautiful and peaceful place to spend time browsing antique shops, enjoying lunch or dinner in one of its fine restaurants, or enjoying a play in one of the old, beautiful theaters. Because we had decided at the last minute, we didn't have any hotel reservations. Because we were so familiar with the area due to our many past trips, we felt confident that once we arrived we would find accommodations without any trouble. We knew when we arrived in Jefferson, that there were two Best Western hotels. One, in Jefferson and the other approximately twenty miles outside of town. We had stayed in the one the farthest away before, so we thought this trip we would stay in the town itself. Upon entering the lobby of the motel in Jefferson, we were greeted half-way to the registration counter by a middle-aged woman, who asked in a very stern and commanding voice, "Do you folks have a reservation?" We replied that we didn't, but sure would appreciate it if she could accommodate us anyway. All the while she was conversing with us, she never looked up from the paper she was reading. Finally, after what seemed an eternity, she said she probably could find us a smoking room, even though we'd asked her for a non-smokers room. Janet and I looked at each other, then very politely asked if we might inspect the room before making a decision. We knew that some smok-

Have a good attitude and have a good life.

ers rooms carried odors that neither of us could tolerate, while others weren't as bad. The woman then informed us, again while reading her paper in the same stern voice as before, that we could not look at the room before making our decision. She seemed angered and her face flushed at our request. We then politely declined her room and left without hesitating another moment.

When we got back to the car, Janet started laughing. Because she knows me so well, she knew that the minute the lady started talking rudely that we were not going to be staying there. She knows that if someone's rude to me, especially if I'm the customer, there is no chance that I'm going to buy that service or product from them. We then headed towards the hotel twenty miles out of Jefferson. When we arrived, we were pleasantly greeted by a young lady who immediately informed us, that even though we did not have a reservation, she had a lovely room she thought we would enjoy very much. Her next statement had Janet and myself actually laughing out loud. "Would you like to inspect it first, sir?" When we told her that wouldn't be necessary, she started to write up the registration. As she did so, she chatted on about all the activities going on that weekend that we might possibly be interested in. What a difference! What a pleasant attitude! What a delightful person to come into contact with and she helped make our entire weekend a complete joy!

What was it that made these two ladies with the same job responsibilities have two such directly opposing effects on our lives? Nothing more than their attitude! Have a good attitude and have a good life. It

First, get physically active doing something!

doesn't take much to figure out which woman enjoys her life more. (P.S. Our beautiful room was $20.00 less than the one we turned away from.)

We all know that a bad or negative attitude puts you into a bad mood, and a bad mood discourages you from taking any positive action. The question that now needs to be addressed is how do you change a bad attitude or mood into a good and productive one? Everyone is different and one exercise that may work for one person, may not work for another. I'd like to suggest a few exercises for you to try. Find the one that works best for you and use it whenever you need to.

The first thing you should do is examine why you are in this mood and have this attitude. Examine it's source and what exactly brought it on. Was it something that someone said to you? Are you tired? Do you have low energy? Was it something that happened to you earlier in the day? Are you unhappy about something? Do you feel discouraged or afraid of something? Whatever it is, you may even want to determine on a scale of one to ten, just how important the source or reason for your bad attitude. In the final analysis, if the reason has a small number, discard it for what it is, of little importance in the overall scheme of things. If the number is high, acknowledge it and pledge yourself to address it by making steps towards a resolution. Next, examine the five recommendations listed below and see which ones can work for you.

First, get physically active doing something, anything. I don't care what it is. Wash your car, clean your closet, repair something in your garage, rake leaves, anything. Get your hands busy and let your mind

"Idle hands are a devil's
workshop."

Get quiet with yourself
and God.

regroup. My mother had a saying when I was a child that she used to recite when she saw me or my brothers and sisters weren't doing anything. She said, "Idle hands are a devil's workshop." Thanks, Lucy.

Second, get quiet with yourself and God. Meditation time or quiet time has always been a great rebuilding tool for mankind for many, many centuries. Get by yourself in a quiet room. Sit in a comfortable chair with a relaxed posture and let your mind relax. Don't think of anything or anyone. No mind pictures, no looking for answers to anything. No nothing. Just let go and let God take over. He will send the answers for you.

Third, sit down with a good book in your favorite chair and do about fifteen to thirty minutes of reading. Pick an uplifting book such as a motivational book or the Bible. It's impossible to have a bad thought or a bad attitude after reading and concentrating on a good book. Always have some good books around, readily available for you at any time. If you have to go look for a good book at these times you certainly will not find one.

Fourth, listen to a good motivational and uplifting cassette tape or CD. Make sure it is by a speaker you know and respect. Concentrate on what the speaker is saying and maybe even take a few notes for future reference. Have a cassette or CD player, tape or CD, and pad and pencil ready for these occasions, have the tools in a handy place and ready to use.

Fifth, get around some positive people. Surround yourself with people who are excited about life and what they are doing. The feeling is contagious and you

"10-minute miracle."

After only ten minutes, you
have pushed yourself to a new
threshold of confidence.

will soon adopt their character. Such people always seem to be in a great frame of mind. Make those people your friends. This is why business functions are so important to your self development.

Now you have five possible exercises to help you change your mood or attitude. Force yourself, if necessary, to use one of them. Understand that sometimes you will have to force yourself in order to change your mood or attitude. Sometimes it's not easy to do, but you have to in order to make good things happen. If by chance none of these remedies work for you, I have one last sure-fire solution that will surely produce great results. We all know that procrastination is one of the biggest reasons we fail to accomplish our goals. You have to use what I call my "10-minute miracle." If there is something you have been putting off, making a phone call, doing a presentation, attempting to approach a prospect, studying material, or anything you are afraid to start, for whatever reason, just say to yourself, "I'm going to start on this project for ten minutes." If, at the end of that ten minutes I want to stop, I can without a guilty conscious. If at the end of ten minutes of your best effort you have the same feelings, quit. Just quit! Just stop what you're doing and don't attempt to go on. You can quit and not feel bad about it. But you know what? You're going to find out that in most cases that the "thing" you have been putting off, is finally getting done. Yes! Getting done! Why? Because sometimes the hardest thing to achieve is just getting started, and that "thing" turned out not to be anything that you had imagined, or had any real reason to be afraid of. After only ten minutes, you have pushed yourself to a new threshold of confidence. Ten

"Most people make a
mountain out of a molehill."

Success is a fulfilled objective
of a focused, determined,
fortified, and energized person.

minutes into the project you have found out that you could do this "thing" that previously had been stopping you. It was nothing compared to what you had been telling yourself.

My mother had another saying (I'm sure yours said it too), "most people make a mountain out of a molehill." Let's make a molehill out of any imagined mountain.

Concentration is the next key element to being successful. When I say concentration, I mean the ability, determination, and stamina to stay focused on your defined goal to be successful. Success is not a happenstance thing that just comes along to some people and ignores others. Success is a fulfilled objective of a focused, determined, fortified, and energized person, who will not take any result that does not lead to their eventual goal. So if that is the case, why is it that some people can do it and others find it so difficult? If this has been one of your challenges, let's examine some of the possible reasons. As you evaluate and score yourself in the following exercise, be frank, open-minded, and honest in your personal evaluation. Acknowledge with a highlighter any or all of the possible villains in your quest for success.

Self-appraisal Exercise

1. Do I fully complete tasks and projects?

2. Do I rehearse positive results in my mind?

3. Do I have habits that need to be changed?

4. Do I keep my career goals constantly in my mind?

5. Do I keep positive thoughts?

Do I worry too much about the consequences of failure or the rewards of success?

Everything you have ever done in your life first started with a thought.

6. Is it difficult for me to stay focused on a specific task?

7. Do I allow other people to influence me?

8. Do I have too many projects going on at the same time?

9. Do I worry too much about the consequences of failure or the rewards of success?

10. In my heart and mind, do I really have a burning desire for success?

Let's examine each one of these individually, starting with the first one:

Do I fully complete tasks and projects? If your answer is no, then ask yourself why not? Is it because you're satisfied with the amount accomplished? Does it seem hopeless to pursue on? Do you start on another project before the present one is completed? Or, is it possible you just lose interest? I don't know your reasons; however, the minute you understand and identify them you then are on your way to correcting them.

Do I rehearse positive results in my mind? Why is an affirmative "yes!" so important? Everything you have ever done in your life first started with a thought, the person you married, the house or car you bought, the job or career you chose, even the clothes you are wearing. Your thoughts become tangible things in your life. Does this also hold true for success? Absolutely! It's extremely important to rehearse positive conclusions to your success goals. If what you think about comes to pass, then it is vital you think, in a positive fashion, the results you want to obtain in your network marketing career.

These habits do not have to be
bad habits.

Would you prefer to have
pleasing habits or
pleasing results?

Do I have habits that need to be changed? If you have acquired habits that are inhibiting your success, first, be honest with yourself and acknowledge them. Identify when, how, and why you acquired these habits. Recognize and acknowledge that they are possible reasons you are not succeeding in your career goals. Remember, these habits do not have to be bad habits in the way we normally define them. They may be pleasant habits, such as going to the movies on a regular basis, watching certain television programs each week, having a night out with friends on occasion, belonging to a sport team that participates in scheduled events, or even cutting your grass every Saturday. Good or bad, these habits have the same effect on your success—they take away from it! Certainly all bad habits should be recognized, dealt with, and eliminated from your life. However, what about some of those pleasant habits we just mentioned? Are they also derailing your success? The answer, unfortunately, is yes! How can a pleasant habit take me away from achieving success? The answer is simple—Time. Time that you spend is taken away from your desired goal. Now, you may say to yourself, "I don't care. I like doing these things and I'm going to keep on doing them!" However, if you truly have a burning desire to succeed, then the right answer comes in the form of a question: Would you prefer to have pleasing habits or pleasing results? You cannot have both. Pleasing habits may add fun and joy to your existence, but many times they add nothing to achieving success. You be the judge. Pleasing results should be your goal!

Do I keep my career goals constantly in my mind? This question presents a challenge that, if accepted,

Success becomes simple
when you understand the
correct laws.

will reap huge rewards for you. Do you keep your career goals constantly in your mind? The correct answer is, you must! If you believe Jesus Christ when he said, "As man thinketh in his heart, so shall he be." If you believe Earl Nightingale when he said, "You become what you think about," you must! If you believe Denis Waitley when he said, "Man moves in the direction of his current dominant thoughts," you must keep your career goals constantly in your mind to have them manifest into your life. It's law! The same law that has the sun coming up each morning. The same law that has the moon in the sky each night. The same law that brings the tide in and out each day. The same law of gravity, that says objects fall to the ground not rise to the sky. Once you understand these laws, honor and bond them to yourself and in your life, all and every good goal can and will be yours to enjoy.

Do I keep positive thoughts? Just as an exercise let's reverse the process and keep negative thoughts in our mind. If what we have just said and agreed to is law, then the same law holds true for negative thoughts. They too will become fact and real in your life. Success becomes simple when you understand the correct laws.

Is it difficult for me to stay focused on a specific task? Could this be one of your short comings? If it is, remember the old wise tale: Jack of all trades, master of none. Is this you? Remember, you cannot be the best handyman, the best bowler, the best TV watcher, or the best grass cutter, and the best network marketer building a successful business.

Do I allow other people to influence me? This question

Are we, as network marketers going through life with a plac- ard on our bodies?

God should always be number one on anyone's list.

brings attention to how other people can influence us and our lives. Without a doubt, people who are in the network marketing business are open to and the subject of more free (but not asked for) advice and counsel than any other business or endeavor. What is it that makes any person, family or friend, think we are looking for their approval or blessing to get into this type of business? Why do they think it is their mission in life to give their opinion on our chances of success, especially when most of it is so negative? Are we, as network marketers going through life with a placard on our bodies that invites just about anyone to take their best shot at us? Don't they realize just how negative they come across? What is it about their lives that they feel they have the right to do this? I don't know. Possibly the thought that since they don't care to pay the price for success, they become jealous of anyone who does. Let's not become like them, and at the same time, let's not allow anyone to influence our lives in a negative way.

Do I have too many projects going on at the same time? If you have too many projects going on at the same time, you need to sit down with your spouse and determine what really is important to you and your future. Do a simple exercise, write down a list of everything you are presently doing. Then, prioritize your list by importance. Remember, if your business is not near the top of that list, you probably won't become more successful. I have always taught that God should always be number one on anyone's list. Without a strong belief in God and His Laws, you cannot be successful. I personally also believe that your family or loved ones should be number two on your

If you have to ask yourself...

list. Without people to share with and love, what is the purpose of life? I would suggest that your successful business or career be number three. Some people may argue with me that number two and number three should be reversed, arguing that without a successful business, you cannot take care of your family in a loving way. They do have a strong point, but I'll stick to my list. As far as outside activities or projects are concerned, if you have to ask yourself, "are these important enough to me to take time out of my life to do, even if they might be stealing the time I might be spending on building my network career?" They are most likely a deterrent. You should eliminate them and concentrate on what is important to you.

Do I worry too much about the consequences of failure or the rewards of success? One of the greatest and to the point stories I have ever heard, tells of a motivational speaker offering to pay an individual $10, if he can simply walk the length of a beam that is fifteen feet long and 8 inches wide without stepping off the beam. The beam is resting on the ground and to earn the $10, all that person has to do is walk and balance himself the length of the beam. I think you will agree, that this would present no problem for just about anyone who can walk and has a normal sense of balance. An easy $10.00 right? No real fear or consequence of failure exists for stepping off the beam onto the floor, except maybe losing the $10.00. But what if we up the ante to $1,000 and the beam is raised between two 15-story buildings? Falling would mean certain death. Now, the element of fear enters into the equation. We were able to walk on that beam when it was on the ground with absolutely no problem. But

The possibility of
negative consequences
takes command.

You will allow nothing to stop
you.

when we took that same beam and just elevated it, immediately we start thinking about the consequences of failure, and hesitate to take that first step. The same thing happens and in many cases actually stops some people from attempting to build a business or a network of distributors. The same thoughts of failure enter into their minds even in making a phone appointment or offering their business opportunity to prospects. They think that they may be turned down and then they would feel disappointed and embarrassed and would therefore be a failure. So you see, there again the possibility of negative consequences takes command. In order to overcome this thought process, you must think and dwell on the rewards of possible success. For example: when making an appointment or offering the business plan, you should be telling yourself that this appointment or new distributor is a result of your efforts and is going to turn into a new "key" or very valuable distributor in your network. Possibly even someone who will bring hundreds or even thousands of new distributors to your organization. With that kind of positive thinking you will make that phone call or excellent sales presentation. You will allow nothing to stop you. A good exercise for overcoming your fears about making phone calls or presentations of your business plan, is to tell yourself that the person on the other end of the phone or listening to you across the table could quite possibly be the one key person to building a tremendous leg in your business. From this day forward, never allow yourself to think or dwell on the possible results of failure. Think and say to yourself that your next task, whatever it may be, will be an extremely valuable

Concentrate on one bird and
get your limit.

In your heart and mind,
do you really have a burning
desire for success?

key in your future and is going to help you reach your desired goal.

In order to drive home my point on the importance of concentrating on your goal, I'd like to share a personal story with you. As a teenager, I loved to go quail hunting in the hills and brush country of Indiana, where I grew up. Not having the luxury of a good bird dog, I often found myself right in the middle of a covey of quail when they flushed up around me. If you have ever had done this, you know what I mean when I say, at first, you are totally surprised, startled, a little scared, and totally unprepared. Your first instinct when you see all those birds, is to just start firing away thinking that with all those birds, you're bound to hit one of them! Well, almost always when I did that the results were the same. As we used to say back in Indiana, I was skunked! No birds. My brother Jim, an experienced hunter, later taught me that all I have to do is pick out a specific bird and follow that bird's flight with my sights, squeeze the trigger, and I would have much better results. No truer advice was ever given a young hunter. "Concentrate on one bird and get your limit. In Indiana your limit was five quail. In network marketing your limit numbers in thousands..." Concentration is truly a key ingredient to success.

In your heart and mind, do you really have a burning desire for success? You have to ask yourself this question because without a true burning desire you will never achieve your objective. Now, the only way I can help you here is possibly to define the term "burning desire" so that you can fully appraise your own determination and the depth that you can generate

You will not allow anything or
anyone to stop you!

in your cause. So what exactly does "burning desire" mean? Or better yet, what should it mean to you? First, if you have this "burning desire" nothing can or will stop you from achieving. Now to what intensity must you have this trait?

My brother Bill tells a story about Socrates, the Greek philosopher and teacher, in his lectures. Socrates was asked by one of his young students, how could he acquire knowledge? Without answering. Socrates walked the young lad down to a nearby lake. Then, sitting at the bank of the lake with the student beside him, Socrates thrust the boy's head under the water, holding it against all the struggle, force, and might the young student could generate. It appeared the boy would drown. Bubbles were coming up to the surface and the boy struggled less and less. At what appeared to be the last moment of life for the boy, Socrates released him and pulled his head out of the water. Water spewed from his mouth and he gasped for breath. Socrates then asked the boy, what he desired most when his head was under the water and about to drown? The young student answered: "air air air." Socrates then instructed the boy that when he wanted knowledge as much as he just wanted air, he would have it. That's what I mean by "burning desire." When you want that much desire and intensity for success, you will then have it. You will not allow anything or anyone to stop you!

You must acknowledge that your *attitude* will control and influence your objectives. Acknowledge that a bad attitude can be reversed by the methods that we have discussed. *Concentration* is a must to succeed.

When you have that type of
desire and intensity for success,
you will then have it.

You must focus on what you desire. Identify and correct what's stopping you from staying focused. Without a good and positive attitude and without the ability to concentrate or stay focused, you will not achieve the success you desire.

If God be for us, who can be against us?

Chapter Eight
Belief

In pursuing the ingredients needed to build yourself into a successful network distributor, *belief* has to be one of your strongest attributes. Without an unfailing sense of belief success will become an improbability. Don't try and fool yourself into thinking otherwise.

You may acquire, fortify, equip, improve on, and learn all of the other tangibles that are needed to become successful in this book, but without an unshakable sense of *belief,* success cannot come into your life.

In order to understand and appreciate the depth of what I mean, let's take a look at history and the men and women who have impacted it with a personal demonstration of action, courage, and belief, realizing that their belief enabled them to achieve their ultimate goals and desires.

Abraham Lincoln provides an excellent example. Lincoln, like so many people, tried to find success by traveling many different career paths. Each of his attempts, some failures and many successes, paved the way to the next challenge ultimately ending with him being elected president of the United States, and being

"A sweet sense of confidence
and belief crept into his soul."

credited with saving the Union. Career stops along for Lincoln included navigator for a riverboat, store merchant, volunteer Indian fighter, postmaster, surveyor, circuit lawyer, state politician, and private attorney. Each result, whether it be good or bad, built belief for his next challenge to come.

Lincoln's supreme test of belief came in July 1863, at the battle of Gettysburg during the Civil War. General Lee, commander of the Southern forces, marched his army of 73,000 seasoned soldiers into Pennsylvania for the battle that would later determine the outcome of the war. Lee's men had just come off some very successful campaigns and were feeling confident of their abilities to prevail in the upcoming battle. This was the first battle of any magnitude to be fought on Northern soil. The fear and anxiety of the Northern population was akin to frenzy and near panic-stricken. Lincoln, aware of the gravity of the situation and the consequences of the outcome, is said to have gone into his private quarters and prayed to God for a victory at Gettysburg. He later stated he turned over to God the cause and told Him that this war was His also. Lincoln then prayed that if He would stand by the Union soldiers, Lincoln would stand by Him. President Lincoln later stated that when he left the room, a "sweet sense of confidence and belief" crept into his soul, and he then knew the outcome of the battle would be favorable. Lincoln's advisors and generals were stunned and amazed at his strong sense of belief and his calm demeanor. As we know from history, even though both sides suffered tremendous losses, the North was credited with a major victory that lead to the conclusion of the war. The states were

Power of an unyielding sense of belief.

reunited into one government and we became the United States of America.

What the history books don't tell us, is that Abraham Lincoln, after his death, became a revered man the world over. He was admired and respected for his works, writings, morals, and, most of all, for his beliefs. What most people still do not realize, is that since his death, Abraham Lincoln is the most written about person with the exception of Jesus Christ.

I believe this is a perfect example of the power of an unyielding sense of belief.

"If God be for us, who can be against us?" Romans 8.

Another example of an individual with world class belief is Charles A. Lindbergh. Lindbergh was born in 1902 and raised on his parents' farm in Minnesota. His early years were influenced by his parents' farm with all of its farm machinery, his grandfather's laboratory in Detroit, Michigan, with all the electrified motors, telescopes, liquids that could dissolve metal and so on, and his many trips to Washington, D.C. where his father served ten years in Congress. Of these three influences, the politics of Washington interested him the least.

In 1912 he attended his first air show and almost immediately aviation attracted him above all else. He attended flying school and at the age of twenty-one bought his first airplane, a World War I salvage trainer. With this airplane he earned a meager living as a barnstormer. It was about this time in his life that he enlisted in the Army, as an Air Cadet. Upon graduation, he became an Air Mail Chief Pilot, flying the route

"Faith is to believe what we do not see; and the reward of this faith, is to see what we believe."

between St. Louis and Chicago. He later revealed that it was at this time in his life, that he first envisioned a non-stop flight between New York and Paris across the Atlantic ocean, considered virtually impossible at the time.

What kind of belief would one have to have to attempt an undertaking of such magnitude? Belief in the airplane. Belief in the preparation for such a challenge. Belief in his support people, but most importantly, what depth of belief did Lindbergh have in himself and his abilities to even attempt such an undertaking? A belief so strong and unparalleled that even the safety and concern for his own life could not stop him. Lindbergh not only accomplished this historic flight in thirty-three hours in 1927, but went on to become a highly successful businessman, and a consultant to the Ford Motor Company. He was well renowned and respected in the field of aviation and became a test pilot. He was later made a Brigadier General in the Air Force. In his later years, he dedicated most of his life to conservation and wildlife preservation. He was an American hero his entire adult life. What a life! What great accomplishments! What a man! What a belief!

"Faith is to believe what we do not see; and the reward of this faith, is to see what we believe." St. Augustine.

Bill Gates, chairman and co-founder of the megagiant, Micro Soft Empire, is another outstanding example of what can be accomplished with an unlimited abundance of belief and specialized knowledge.

The story is worth retelling to illustrate the value of

The sermon on the mount.

these two traits with special emphasis on the power of belief. Bill Gates was born to Mary and Bill, Jr., intelligent and successful people. His mother was a teacher with a flair for being associated with successful and influential people. His father Bill, Jr., became an attorney after serving in the army during World War II as a first lieutenant. Bill, Jr. was intelligent and ambitious and became a very successful attorney in the Seattle area.

Bill Gates, III, was born in October, 1955, the second child of the marriage. From a very early age, Bill III demonstrated unusual qualities of energy and intelligence. It is recorded that he read the entire *World Book Encyclopedia* by the age of eight. He had an obsessive personality, and a compulsive need to be the best at whatever he attempted. His grandmother on his mother's side pushed him to read books and to excel in all his endeavors.

For example his minister, Reverend Turner, challenged young Bill's confirmation class to learn and recite without error; chapters 5, 6, and 7 of the book of Matthew (the sermon on the mount). The reward was a trip and dinner at the top of the Space Needle Tower, which is a landmark in the Seattle area. Bill III not only did it, but was flawless to the point of perfection. It was something that had never been done before in Reverend Turner's class.

His early interest in computers was revealed at a Boy Scout jamboree. As a scout, he was required to do a presentation around the campfire one night. All the other scouts had done the customary knot-tying, tree and leaf identification, and normal scout skills. Bill III

"Learn from people smarter
than myself."

and his friend had other ideas. They did a demonstration and presentation on what computers could do. At that time, little was known about computers and its possible capabilities. Here was a young Boy Scout and his friend doing just this. From this early age, it is easy to tell that young Bill had a vision.

At the age of eleven, Bill III was enrolled in a school for the gifted. In this environment his desire for more knowledge about computers was cultivated. Computers were still relatively obscure. There were no books, libraries, or sources of information about computers readily available. Anyone interested in computers had to search for any information, which Bill III did with an intense and voracious appetite. It did not take long before other students and even people in the computer business sought out Bill for his expertise and knowledge in computers. His name was well known on campus for his knowledge of computers and their innerworkings. Bill III and an upper classman, Paul Allen, joined together because of their common curiosity about computers. While students at the Lakeside Private School together, they tried all kinds of money making ventures. They computerized student enrollment for the school, wrote payroll and tax information software for private companies, and many other self-generating tasks of employment. Their two goals were simple and straightforward—to learn more about computers and figure out a way for that knowledge to pay them huge returns.

Upon graduation, Bill III entered Harvard University to, in his words, "Learn from people smarter than myself." It is said that at this time Bill and his part-

Big belief...big reward.

ner, Paul Allen, had vowed to realize certain dreams together. They were (1) to obtain in depth knowledge about computers, (2) to make big money, and (3) to maintain an unbelievable sense of belief within themselves to make it happen. Looking back, you know that these two young boys were on a sure path to success.

Their big break came with a company called Mits in Albuquerque, New Mexico. They wanted to adapt a new computer language called "BASIC" to their computer, called "Altair," which the engineers at Mits thought nearly impossible. From an article in an electronics publication, Bill III and Paul Allen learned of this situation. While they did not have the solution, they phoned Mits and informed them that they indeed had such a program that could link these two entities together. Because they had such complete belief in themselves, their abilities, and with eight weeks of intense work on this project, they were able to complete and successfully achieve this goal. The personal computer revolution had begun!

From this accomplishment, fueled by an unbelievable sense of belief, Microsoft was born and was well on its way to becoming the giant empire it is today. (Footnote: Bill Gates III became the youngest billionaire in the history of this country!)

Big belief...big reward.

If ever there was an optimum of a human being, who has demonstrated with their entire life every day, day in and day out, this quality of faith and belief in their cause, this next example sets herself above even this level.

Not once has she ever faltered or doubted the outcome or her purpose and reason.

Mother Teresa is on even a higher plane than all modern day humanity. She has been called a modern day saint and she has emerged herself in the common face of mankind and identified herself with human suffering and privation. Because of her commitment and devotion to her belief, she is known and loved the world over. What is so amazing about her level of belief is that it has been tested not once or twice, but many times over. Her faith and belief in her cause has been and is still tested every day of her life. Not once has she ever faltered or doubted the outcome or her purpose and reason.

In order to really appreciate Mother Teresa, you need to know a little of her beginning and personal history. She was born in 1910 in Yugoslavia of Albanian parents. She was one of three children and was named Agnes. As a teenager, she attended a government school where she joined a Catholic church group called Sodality. This was a devotional and charitable organization. At the age of eighteen, she was sent to India to begin her novitiate where her name was changed for the order in which she partook. She went on to teach geography and later became the principal of St. Mary's High School in Calcutta.

One day she was sent out away from her convent and her entire life and purpose was changed forever. On this rare day, she was exposed to the poor, the dying, the forgotten people on the streets of the city. What she witnessed was the degradation of humanity in its sorriest state. People who were starving, injured, diseased, had no family or had been left alone to die without love or concern.

The only acceptable answer is
the God life spirit that dwells
within all of God's children.

When she returned to the convent, she immediately went to her superior and asked for permission to go out on the streets to administer to the people's needs. You must understand her convent and school life had been happy times with all the conveniences the outside world did not have. She was asking to go into the streets with no place to live and to administer to the poorest of the poor, dying from the cruelest infections known to mankind with no money and no support from anyone.

What was it that stirred this desire in this woman? The only acceptable answer is the God life spirit that dwells within all of God's children. The same spiritual power that God put inside you and me to accomplish any worthwhile goal. How could we ever doubt and not believe in ourselves? If God put it there, who can destroy it? Permission was granted to her to carry on the course she set for herself. She went into the streets of Calcutta and into the lives and hearts of millions. She established shelters where the dying could die surrounded with love, care and compassion. She founded nursing quarters where the sick could be nursed and return to health with loving care. She recruited others to join her in her mission to expand to other cities of need. She started a colony for the lepers and administered to their needs.

For all her amazing grace and accomplishments throughout her life, she asked nothing in return. She has even requested that no one even write about her personally, but that they may write and speak about her efforts against the poverty, sickness, and devastation that goes on in the world. She has devoted her

But faith and belief, to be true
has to be a given love.

entire life to this cause and grants permission to anyone that would want to speak or write of this in the hopes that it will bring awareness to others. This type of "messenger" came in the form of a Mr. Malcom Muggeridge. He has quoted her as saying "Christ's life was not written during His lifetime, yet He did the greatest work on earth—he redeemed the world and taught mankind to love His Father. The work is His work and to remain so, all of us are but His instruments who do our little bit and pass by."

During the time that Mr. Muggeridge spent with Mother Teresa, a kind of miracle happened that no one has been able to explain, except that it is the direct result of a person that has lived an extraordinary life. A crew was filming the actual events of day-to-day life in the home for the dying. It was so dimly lit that everyone filming was concerned that you would not even be able to make out anyone in the pictures. When the crew took it back to be developed, they were shocked and astonished to find that not only could you see it clearly, but that it produced a glowing light. The film crew could never identify the origin of this light.

Because of her overwhelming sense of *belief,* dedication and extreme hard work, Mother Teresa will be revered and looked upon as a truly modern day saint for years to come.

"Faith and belief is lacking, because there is so much selfishness and so much gain for self. But faith and belief, to be true has to be a given love. Love, faith and belief go together. They complete each other." Mother Teresa.

When you have complete
belief, your every thought will
be directed to your success
and nothing short will be
accepted.

Now that we have revisited, experienced, and hopefully appreciated the accomplishments of these four outstanding people and more importantly have a truer understanding of the depth of their beliefs, let's examine where we need to have that same type of unfailing character. You see, it is not enough to have a feeling of belief about yourself only. You must have that belief in your *goals, business plan, product line, sponsor,* and the *opportunity* that all these together can make possible.

I would like you to sit down with your spouse and examine each of these specific areas individually and share your thoughts, concerns, and beliefs. If you should have some doubts, express them now. Listen closely to each other and take down some notes stating your strong and weak areas. It's extremely important to have a complete understanding and insight into each other's most intimate thoughts, fears, and doubts (if any). Bring them to the surface. Remember, any of these will unconsciously stop you from pursuing with the necessary intensity. Remember: A problem identified, is a problem half solved. One of the worst things you can do is to proceed in a half-hearted fashion, simply because you will achieve half-hearted results. When you have complete belief, your every thought will be directed to your success and nothing short will be accepted. Make sure your goals are congruent with your spouse's. If they are not, your courses of action will be different. It's like pulling a wagon in different directions; a lot of energy will be expelled, but you will gain very little distance. Being partners in your business and having an equal shared spirit and belief will accomplish everything. The combined energy and

Both partners need to join forces to get out of the starting gate.

synergism of a unified couple cannot be stopped from achieving their goals.

In reality, it's no different than the example of the horse pulling contest of the old county fair days, when it was discovered that if one horse could pull a sled loaded with 2,000 pounds, two horses could pull a similar sled with 5,000 or 6,000 pounds through their combined efforts. Couples that enter into the network marketing business at different levels of belief retard their chances of success and have a more difficult start up. We have all heard stories where one partner was all fired up and the other was less enthusiastic, and only when both joined forces did things really start happening for them. I might mention here, that it takes an extremely believing and committed person to single-handedly start up and carry on a successful business, while the other partner is indifferent or even negative about it. Both partners need to join forces to get out of the starting gate. If you are the noncommitted partner in this new start up business, do one thing: don't destroy your spouse's belief, enthusiasm, or dream with your negative thoughts or expressions of doubt. Give him or her a chance to explore the possibilities. If you feel you cannot help build, don't tear down or attempt to destroy their dreams for a new lifestyle for your family. What you may find is that the possibilities and opportunities are everything and even more than even your partner envisioned. You can then join in the building process without bringing some unwanted baggage of past comments, lack of support, and negativity into the partnership. In other words, you start clean and can be of an immediate asset. Now, let's explore some ways you and your partner can build belief.

"Knowledge is power."

You build yourself and your
belief from your past successes.

As I have said in the earlier chapters, "knowledge is power." It empowers you to be strong, confident, and dynamic. It is that in-depth source of knowledge that fortifies your belief. In-depth knowledge eliminates fears, such as making phone calls for appointments, personal contacts, plan presentations to couples or groups, or the like. When you eliminate fear, it is immediately replaced with belief and confidence about all those vital areas that are so important to your success. So whatever you are afraid of, in whatever area of this business, gather and seek out knowledge about that specific thing. And when you do, the fear will vanish and you will become a stronger, more confident, and believing person, who is well on the path to fulfilling your goals.

A major way to build belief within yourself is by successfully completing some small task or project that you have pushed yourself to attempt. It acts like a building block—one block at a time—proving to yourself that you're capable and can do it. Then, you are able to take on more difficult and challenging endeavors. You build yourself and your beliefs from your past successes. Remember, it's important to start with smaller tasks or challenges, ones that you have a greater chance to accomplish. Don't bite off more than you can chew.

Several years ago, I conducted commercial selling workshops for the largest and most successful direct sales company in the world. One of my pieces of advice for aspiring commercial distributors was to start with small prospects. When you start small you have a much better chance to succeed. The small prospects

Today is truly the first day of the
rest of your life.

attracted less salespeople, therefore, less competition. This enables you to work through your sales presentation, and if you were to make a mistake it would be no big tragedy. However, if you were successful and got an order, all at once your confidence and belief level escalated, taking you up to the next level. Remember— you build your belief patterns from your own past successful accomplishments. You also build your disbelief patterns from your own past failed endeavors.

Before we proceed, you need to understand and believe one very important thought. It doesn't matter what you have done in the past. It doesn't matter how much money you have made. It doesn't hatter what education level you have. It doesn't matter what your color or nationality is. The only thing that matters is what you are going to do *now,* today with this new opportunity. *Today* is truly the first day of the rest of your life.

So what we have learned thus far is that one method to create belief is by recognizing doubts and fears and replacing them with positive knowledge about your new endeavor. A second way to establish belief is by seeking out and building relationships with people already in the business. It is vital to consult people only in the business, because others may be prejudiced, or not qualified in their opinions. Attend meetings, rallies, and functions regularly. Build a relationship with people who are similar to you. People who have the same goals and dreams. Make yourself a list of issues that concern you, or where you need more information. Find out how long your new acquaintances have been in the business, their plan of

It's an investment of time and
energy well spent that may
produce great returns.

"Hardware story."

action, how much time they dedicate to their business, what some of their concerns are, what have they accomplished so far, and so on. What's working best for them may, or may not, work for you, but find out by gathering information. It's an investment of time and energy well spent that may produce great returns. I have always been an advocate of seeking out knowledge and information on any new project. It better qualifies me and helps me be more successful in my pursuits. One thing to remember is that the people you seek knowledge from, should have basic similarities to you so that you might mirror and match them. People who do not have basic similarities to you, will make it nearly impossible for you to duplicate their efforts and results.

To summarize this chapter, we have come to better appreciate these four examples of strong people who have demonstrated an extraordinary amount of *belief* in accomplishing their own individual goals. We have also explored different ways and methods to build this sense of belief within ourselves and our lives. Hopefully, you now understand the necessity of being able to create this same characteristic within yourself to achieve your own goals.

If you still have some confusion or doubts about mastering belief within yourself, think about this example. I call it my "hardware story." Being a homeowner, it seems that there is always some project or task that I need to take care of around the house, such as fixing a leaking pipe, putting up a shelf, installing a bookcase, or any number of things that we all do to take care of our home. Whenever I start one of these

No trips back to the supply store.

projects it always seems that I need some supplies from the hardware store to complete it. My goal is to make a list of the things I'll need and make just one trip to the hardware store. What I have found is that I almost always need something else, or I forget something and can never make just one trip. To be honest, sometimes I end up making several trips just to complete one project. Does this sound familiar? Point of story: when God created the Earth, everything that mankind was ever going to need was put on the Earth at that time. Everything that early mankind, stone-age mankind, and modern day mankind ever needed was there from the beginning. This miracle is also true for all future mankinds. In other words, God did not forget *anything*. He did a perfect job on his first attempt. *No trips back to the supply store.*

Since God did such a perfect job creating this Earth we live on, do you think for one minute He would settle for anything less than a perfect job in creating you and me? No-way! He didn't forget anything. He put everything inside of us to be anything we want to become. The only thing He asks of us, is to develop ourselves into the best human being possible, developing all the ingredients He bestowed in us. We should become the best human being possible. He asks us to demonstrate, love, care, use our intelligence, show empathy, and, yes, use our belief.

"I'm going to make you a little lower than the angels, with dominion over all things." God, Our Father Almighty.

Take action in the correct areas.

Chapter Nine
Taking Action

We have been trying to identify the characteristics of a successful network distributor, or more importantly, a successful human being. Without question we could have added other intangibles to this list to fully complete the picture. There comes a time, once we acknowledge to ourselves success must come through us, that we begin on the never ending journey of constantly striving to improve ourselves. We must also acknowledge to ourselves that even with these new or improved traits, nothing is going to happen or change in our lives until we, as that new person, *take action* on what we want to accomplish.

We can work on ourselves and build a new and better person, but if we don't do something with this new person, nothing will change in our life. *We must take action* and demonstrate these new and better characteristics to the world and to ourselves. The important thing here is to *take action* in the correct areas. This is the key to real success. Work on, improve, and correct the proper elements to get the proper results. Too many people are mistakenly working on the wrong things and they wonder why they get wrong or unsatisfactory results. It's like the country

Exhibit 1
Distributor Success Rating Scale
A Problem Identified is a Problem Half Solved

Distributor _____

		1	2	3	4	5	6	7	8	9	10
1.	Personal Self Development (Books & Tapes)										
2.	Attitude and Enthusiasm										
3.	Energy Level Plus Health										
4.	Following Upline's System										
5.	Prospecting for New Distributors and Booking Meetings (B.A.M.)										
6.	Show Business Plan Fifteen Times per Month										
7.	Presentation Skills for Showing Business Plan										
8.	Dress Code and Auto Appearance										
9.	Time and Self Management										
10.	Supporting and Attending Local and Major Functions										
11.	Being Goal and Success Oriented										
12.	Being 100 percent Loyal to Your Own Business										
13.	Product Knowledge, Pick-Up, and Delivery										

COMMITMENT TO IMPROVE:

_____ Date: _____

and western song about looking for love in all the wrong places.

Now that you know what you must work on and improve in yourself, I'm going to share with you the right places to apply this new you. You are now going to do a little self analysis to see just where you are at this point in your life. Thirteen important areas are specifically identified to shape and build a successful network marketer. Mastering these thirteen elements will without question assure you of success. As you evaluate yourself, be careful to be as honest as you possibly can be. This is no time to lie to yourself and say you are better than you are. Remember, "A problem identified is a problem half solved." Being as honest and precise as you can be, will pinpoint exactly where you are at this moment.

I want you to judge yourself by putting a check mark in the appropriate box in Exhibit 1. Rate yourself on a scale of 1 to 10 with one as the poorest performance in that category and 10 the best possible performance. If you are not sure how you might rate yourself in one particular area, ask your spouse or sponsor what their appraisal might be. In fact, it would be a good idea, that after you have taken the evaluation test, to have your spouse or upline take the test and appraise you. Compare their test to yours, and see if there are any major differences in any particular area.

Now that you have honestly judged yourself and have rated yourself from one to ten on each criterion *add* the numbers up to get a *total*. Arriving at a total, divide the total by thirteen to get an average.

If your average number is low,
remember, your potential
is high.

For example:

$$
\begin{array}{r}
1.—3 \\
2.—2 \\
3.—4 \\
4.—2 \\
5.—1 \\
6.—4 \\
7.—3 \\
8.—3 \\
9.—2 \\
10.—4 \\
11.—4 \\
12.—4 \\
13.—3 \\
\hline
39
\end{array}
$$

$$39 \div 13 = 3 \text{ average}$$

Now for the first time, you know exactly where you are in the thirteen most important areas to ensure your path to success. For the first time you have taken an inventory of yourself, and know where you presently are on the road to success. You know what you are good at, and also know the areas that need improvement. This is extremely important information. Most people never know, or are able to determine what they may be lacking in order to be successful. Without learning exactly what their strong areas are, as well as their shortcomings, efforts to become successful will prove futile. Identifying your shortcomings gives you an opportunity to correct and improve them and thereby excel.

Exhibit 2
Distributor Success Rating Scale

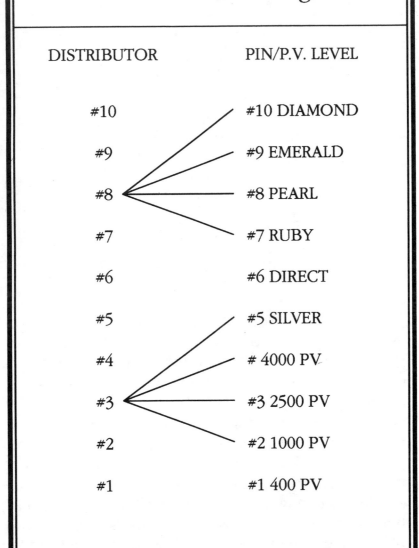

DISTRIBUTOR   PIN/P.V. LEVEL

#10   #10 DIAMOND

#9   #9 EMERALD

#8   #8 PEARL

#7   #7 RUBY

#6   #6 DIRECT

#5   #5 SILVER

#4   # 4000 PV

#3   #3 2500 PV

#2   #2 1000 PV

#1   #1 400 PV

Exhibit 2 shows you how to measure where you are, before you start on a new path to improvement. Based on your evaluation of the thirteen categories, and the average you see exactly at what level you are now. If however, you do not improve and develop yourself, you will have little hope of ever being able to go higher up the chart. Remember, "If you keep on doing what you've always done, you'll keep on getting what you've always got."

If your average came out to eight out of perfect ten score, you now have the potential to become a ruby, pearl, emerald or diamond. Does it really work this way? That's the only way that it *can* work! The more you bring to the table, the more you can take away. If you're not bringing much to the table, then why would you think you have a right to take much away? The great teacher once said, "As ye sow, so shall ye reap." It's that simple!

I believe our purpose on this earth is to improve ourselves and help our fellow man. When we work to accomplish this, we can expect good things to come into our lives. How can they or why should we expect it any other way? If your average number is low, remember, your potential is high.

It is vitally important that you are clear on and understand each of the descriptions in Exhibit 1.

1. *Personal Self Development (Books & Tapes)*. Simply put, are you reading sponsor approved good books and listening to tapes every day? This is where all the information is. Books and tapes contain knowledge, examples, suggestions, and results of other successful people. Remember, "If success is going to

"If success is going to come
to you...it must come
through you."

come to you...it must come *through* you." Very simply put, you have to put "it" inside of you first, and the easiest way to do this is with sponsor or upline approved books and tapes.

Our constant challenge is to continuously build and fortify ourselves into a knowledgeable and better person. You should be listening to tapes every single day or whenever you have an opportunity, while you are in your car between destinations, during a trip, or even just down to the corner market. You never know when a good thought or idea will come into your awareness just because you are listening to tapes. Every day that you grow yourself you become a new and better person. When this happens, ideas that you've missed in the past will suddenly come into your mind that you're reading and listening. You will need to listen to one tape several times over, because you are a different and more aware person each and every new day and you will hear something that you hadn't heard before on the same tape. Learn the tape that you are listening to so that you could recite the thoughts word by word. Learn it so thoroughly, that it is you speaking the words. Then move on to the next dynamic tape or book. This is how you build yourself.

Many people have told me that they have never read books in the past, and it is difficult for them to even get started. I tell them to simply get started! Reading is truly a learned skill. You can teach yourself, but the secret is to discipline yourself to just begin! I do have a few tips. First, find out what time of day you are more alert and can comprehend best. Get comfortable and by yourself with good light and use a high-

"It's good to feel
uncomfortable."

lighter to mark the ideas that sound good to you, so you can refer back later.

The bottom line is that in order to grow and build yourself, you must continuously fortify yourself with new information, and one of the best sources for that is on cassette tapes and in books. You must do whatever is necessary to obtain knowledge. It's as simple as that!

2. *Attitude and Enthusiasm*—see Chapter 7.

3. *Energy Level Plus Health*—see Chapter 2.

4. *Following Upline's System.* One of the most vital keys to success is getting in tune and alignment with your sponsor and their method for building a successful business. In my conversations with so many people who have failed to build their business, there appears to be one common denominator in all of them—they failed to listen to and follow their successful upline's advice and system. They thought they had a better idea or method and by the time they discovered their idea was wrong and not working, they were so confused and disillusioned, they quit! Don't try to reinvent the wheel. If your upline is succeeding and has a tract record for success, get in line with him. Do it his way, even if it's uncomfortable at first for you. Being uncomfortable is good! It means you are doing some things you have not done in the past. You are growing and expanding. One thing I've always told myself: It's good to feel uncomfortable; I'm changing for the better. We need to break out of our comfort zones. The important thing to remember is to follow the advice of you sponsors. Develop personal time with them if at all

You're normal, so don't get
angry with yourself.

possible. While in their presence be a good listener, take notes, seek their advice and suggestions and do what they tell you!

One hard fact to remember, and I don't say this to hurt any feelings, but if you knew the right success principles in the past, you would already be successful and exactly where you want to be in life and in business.

5. *Prospecting for New Distributors and Booking Meetings.* If you are having difficulty picking up the phone and calling a prospect for an appointment, that's okay! Everyone who has ever become successful in this business has experienced those same feelings, and every one after you will also have those fears. You're normal, so don't get angry with yourself. You can overcome this difficulty. Remember and confirm to yourself that you have a great opportunity to share with a new client. In fact, you are doing them a favor by calling and offering them this opportunity. You have the moral duty to offer them a chance to change and enrich their lives for a better future. You have this wonderful concept for building a great business that quite possibly your prospects have been looking for! *You* have just such an opportunity for them. Remember, you are not asking them to buy, you are just asking them to look and evaluate for themselves this exciting opportunity. Tell yourself that the people you are calling need you more than you need them. Make yourself a script for asking for appointments, either writing or typing it out. Don't leave anything to chance. Rehearse the script several times until it sounds natural and flows

Sometimes you have to
"nudge" them a little.

smoothly. When you request an appointment, give the prospect a choice of two possible dates and times that you have open. I call this method a choice of two possible alternatives. It's a win-win situation. You see, it doesn't matter which one they choose. The important thing is that they choose *one!*

One last thing that you need to confirm to yourself before making a call is to tell yourself that you are calling this prospect for the purpose of *helping him* enjoy the chance to change his life for the better. You cannot help your prospects achieve this *until* you have a chance to show them the opportunity. Sometimes you have to nudge them a little in order to help them along. That's okay! They will thank you later.

One last thought. You cannot become successful in the network marketing business, until you master and overcome fear of the telephone. You *can* and *must* do it. As the Nike ad says, *"Just do it!"*

6. *Show Business Plan 15 Times per Month.* Whatever the correct number is for showing your business plan in a month, the bottom line is that it comes down to a matter of numbers. The more times you present your plan to prospects, the better chance you have of adding an associate to your organization. It's that simple! You must make presentations! There are two keys to follow. First, book the meetings—either in your home, coffee shop, or even over lunch—*but book meetings!* Don't be timid or embarrassed to ask a friend or prospect to a meeting. Everybody is looking to improve themselves. Most people don't know how, or where to look, but *you have the how and where!* Second, if you've got

"I'm gonna B.A.M. 'em!"

the meeting or luncheon appointment be sure to make a "great" presentation. Don't waste a meeting with a poor presentation. You will kick yourself later. In my personal selling career, I always thought that if I had an appointment with a client or prospect, I wanted to be sure I prepared a great presentation. Don't be foolish and waste yours or your prospect's time with a poor one. You would be better served if you gave no presentation at all, rather than present a poor one.

In order to book and complete the necessary presentations for success, you must organize your evenings and weekends. Try to figure how you can multiply yourself by getting several prospects to one meeting for one presentation. Remember, the two keys—book lots of presentations and make each presentation the best you are capable of!

Jerry Boggus, an Amway Diamond and friend of mine, gave me a great expression that he uses when he books meetings. Jerry says, "I'm gonna B.A.M. 'em!" (Book A Meeting!)

Sometimes we all need a rallying slogan. Well, let's use Jerry's! Let's B.A.M. 'em!

7. *Presentation Skills for Showing Business Plan*—see Chapter 1.

8. *Dress Code and Auto Appearance.* The great thing about this element to success, is that it's easy and quick to accomplish. How long does it take you to run your car through a car wash?

You know how you feel in a clean car? You feel great! I've always thought that if you feel great you

Dress the best you can
all the time!

have a better chance to do great! A clean car makes a statement about you and what you represent. A clean older car looks newer! A clean car seems to run better! A clean, well-maintained car creates the correct image for new prospects in their appraisal of you. Do I need to say more?

Let's examine your own personal dress code a little more closely. It's my belief that it is impossible to over dress. It's my belief you should always look your best. If you're a gentleman, your best should be a suit, white shirt, and tie. How about a sport coat and tie? That's fine, but a suit and tie are better. I've also been asked about a pastel shirt. Again, that's fine, but white is better. My point is that a gentleman in a dark suit, white shirt, and tie looks successful and projects that image. The last part of the gentleman's picture of success is his shoes. I don't know how many men still shine their own shoes, but I do. I never leave my home or office without shined shoes. Ask any lady their first impression of a gentleman's attire and, in most cases, she will mention the condition of his shoes. Shoes complete the picture of success.

I don't claim to be an expert on women's attire, but I can share my own personal opinions. I appreciate a woman dressed attractively in either a nice dress or blouse and skirt. My personal thought is, that a lady in slacks looks less professional and business-like. However, let me again point out that this is my own personal opinion.

More importantly, remember that many opinions are based on a man's or woman's dress attire. Why not dress the best you can all the time!

> # If you have no loyalty to yourself, who or what do you have loyalty to?

9. *Time and Self Management*—see Chapter 4.

10. *Supporting and Attending Local and Major Functions.* In a new distributor's initial start up time, one of the most difficult decisions to make is spending the money and time attending upline and major functions. It's difficult, certainly, because of the time involved and the necessary money. But the real reason is, that they don't understand the value or what they are going to get out of it. Once we all understand the value received, then we all know it is time and money well spent.

Upline and major functions are a wonderful source of knowledge, ideas, and suggestions to build your business, and there is a never ending supply of good people willing to share all these with you. However, I believe the most important value you can receive, is the consciousness or awareness that you are planting within yourself, by attending the functions. In reality you become a new and better person. You are more aware of all the opportunities and life style you are capable of achieving. You sense it, see it, hear it, and feel it. You become it. You must attend functions to become the new you and to gain the success you desire.

11. *Being Goal and Success Oriented*—see Chapter 6.

12. *Being 100 percent Loyal to Your Own Business.* How is this element a factor in your success? Something so easy as being 100 percent loyal to you or own business is so obvious. If you have no loyalty to yourself, who or what do you have loyalty to?

I believe in all my travels, I've heard just about every *wrong* excuse for such an easy question. For

Penny wise, but pound foolish!

example, "Some of the products are too expensive," "It's too much trouble keeping track of what I may need and then ordering them through my upline," "It's so easy to just go down to the supermarket or drug store when I need something, rather than to order from my upline," "There are some products I just don't like," " What does it matter if I don't buy the products or services? I'm the only one who really knows."

Well, here's my answers to those statements! Why should you care if the products or services are a little more expensive? Would you trade a little extra money spent for a successful business that you can enjoy the rest of your life? My mom had a great statement for this kind of thought process: Penny wise, but pound foolish! For the second excuse, simply make yourself an inventory sheet on the products you normally use in your home each month. Check off the items you need on order day and keep the list inside your pantry. Then turn the order in. The third excuse: everybody is looking for the easy way out. Put a little effort on the important things in your life. There's a good reason why convenience stores do so well these days. They count on people running out of something and not wanting to go through any trouble to get it. People go to convenience stores and pay 30 percent to 40 percent more for a product, rather than planning a little ahead for it. The fourth excuse: if there are some products you do not personally like, simply don't buy them! Just buy *all* the products you like and enjoy. Last and most importantly, "What does it matter? I'm the only one who knows." That's the question and that's the answer! You are not supporting your own business! How can you suggest to an associate they should

If you are going to become a successful business person, you must take action with yourself.

support their business, when you yourself don't support your own? How can you easily and convincingly talk about your products when you don't use them yourself? You have no credibility with anyone, but especially yourself and *you know it!* You must be loyal to your own business!

13. *Product Knowledge, Pick-Up, and Delivery*—see Chapter 1.

The summary for this chapter is very simple. To complete any project or task, *taking action* must be applied to bring that project or task to a successful conclusion. If you are going to become a successful business person, you must take action with yourself.

In this chapter, I have shared with you the thirteen most important areas to take action. I have also given you a method to judge yourself on a scale of 1 to 10 to determine where you are, therefore, identifying the areas you need to improve on.

The rest is up to you! Do you truly in your heart, want success? If your answer is an affirmative *yes,* then you...*need to take action!*

It's now up to you to bond
these principles to yourself
and make them your principles
for life.

Afterward

Congratulations! You have finished this book! That makes a positive statement about you. By searching for the correct success principles, it says that you are a success-minded individual.

I truly believe this book contains many of these success-type principles that you will need to build your life and career. It's now up to you to bond these principles to yourself and make them your principles for life.

There is no question in my mind that when you do, you are well on the path to achieving your goals and desires. Remember, one book and its ideas are not enough ammunition to sustain you in your journey through life. You must continue to search out more information and material to keep you on course. You now know that everything you need to succeed is in you, but you must continuously seek out, fortify, and nurture that part of yourself to become the successful human being you desire.

If our paths should cross at a function or seminar in the future, please come up and say hello!

God bless you!

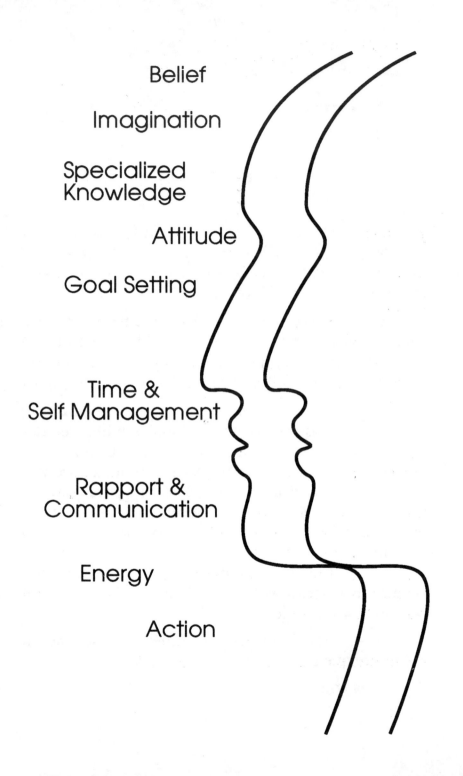

Belief

Imagination

Specialized
Knowledge

Attitude

Goal Setting

Time &
Self Management

Rapport &
Communication

Energy

Action

REMEMBER

"If you are not working on yourself... you are working on the wrong project!"

Jack Stanley

recognizes

_____
Name